Variety®

POWER PLAYERS 2000

POWER PLAYERS 2000

Movers and Shakers, Power Brokers and Career Makers in Hollywood

EDITED BY
Chris Petrikin, Andrew Hindes, AND Dan Cox

INTRODUCTION BY
Peter Bart, Editor in Chief, *Variety*

A PERIGEE BOOK

A Perigee Book
Published by The Berkley Publishing Group
A division of Penguin Putnam Inc.
375 Hudson Street
New York, New York 10014

Book design by Tiffany Kukec
Cover design by Miguel Santana

First edition: December 1999

Published simultaneously in Canada.

The Penguin Putnam Inc. World Wide Web site address is
http://www.penguinputnam.com

Library of Congress Cataloging-in-Publication Data

Variety power players 2000 : movers and shakers, power brokers and career makers in Hollywood / edited by Chris Petrikin, Andrew Hindes, and Dan Cox.— 1st ed.
p. cm.
Includes index.
ISBN 0-399-52569-6
1. Motion pictures—Biography—Dictionaries. 2. Motion pictures—Directories. I. Petrikin, Chris. II. Hindes, Andrew. III. Cox, Dan.

PN1998.2.V35 1999
384'.8'092279494—dc21

99-046974
CIP

Printed in the United States of America

10 9 8 7 6 5 4 3 2 1

CONTENTS

INTRODUCTION

By Peter Bart, Editor in Chief, *Variety* and *Daily Variety*

The first time I was appointed to an important-sounding job in the movie industry (vice president for production at Paramount), I was inundated with the customary congratulatory phone calls from people who hoped to do business with me. The most memorable message, however, came from a man who occupied a similar job at Columbia, a rival studio. His name was Peter Guber, and his message skipped the usual amenities. Instead, he proposed to me the precise terms of the separation agreement (i.e., golden parachute) that I should demand upon being fired. The gist of his message: Despite our fancy titles, none of us should ever forget the fact that we don't own our offices, we're just renting them; that nothing in Hollywood lasts forever—indeed, nothing is as evanescent as power in the movie business.

This incident serves as a helpful subtext to *Variety*'s Power List—a reminder that the people mentioned in the coming pages are important today but may be superfluous tomorrow. In compiling our lists, to be sure, we have made an effort to recognize durability and "staying power." Some of the players on our lists may once have been highly successful, say, as producers or executives, but then went on to achieve a similarly strong career as an agent or manager. In show business, flexibility is a key to achieving a substantial career. You may find yourself blocked on one path, only to find opportunity on another.

Our lists attempt to recognize not only durability, but also talent and leadership. Inevitably, some very smart folks were omitted along the way. We apologize up front for any snubs, advertent or inadvertent. Our intentions were honorable: We were not swayed by the pleas of press agents or other representatives who, upon learning of this effort, attempted to influence our reporters.

On the other hand, there is no handy set of criteria to measure power. In the case of writers, you may try to add up credits, but some of the highest-paid writers in Hollywood are essentially rewrite men who, in some cases, don't want to receive credit for a million-dollar "body-and-fender" job. With directors, a filmmaker who has distinguished himself on one or two films may deserve attention over someone who has been responsible for a dozen utterly forgettable movies. In the same vein, an agent or manager who has played a pivotal role in guiding the career of a major star arguably should rank ahead of another talent representative whose client list is bigger but undistinguished or who wields little if any influence over his clients, bowing instead to the judgment of an attorney or manager.

It is the job of our reporters who helped prepare this book to ferret these things out and exercise their judgment accordingly. Hopefully, the resulting list is accurate and representative. Also, hopefully, not too many of the players listed herein will have moved on to other jobs by the time this book is published. At the very least, a quick read of the career paths and backgrounds of the players mentioned in this volume should provide some helpful insights into these murky questions: How does one prepare for a career in show business? What sort of background offers the best experience?

Read and enjoy.

Peter Bart,
Editor in Chief, *Variety*

EXECS

BARKER, Michael, Tom Bernard, and Marcie Bloom · BLAKE, Jeff · CALLEY, John · CHERNIN, Peter · COOK, Richard · DALY, Robert A., and Terry Semel · DE LUCA, Michael · DI BONAVENTURA, Lorenzo · DOLGEN, Jonathan · FELLMAN, Dan · FISHER, Lucy · FRIEDMAN, Rob · GARNER, Todd, and Nina Jacobson · GILL, Mark · GREENSTEIN, Scott, and Russell Schwartz · HARPER, Robert · LANSING, Sherry · LAW, Lindsay · LEVIN, Robert · LEWELLEN, Wayne · LYNNE, Michael · MACDONALD, Laurie, and Walter Parkes · MALIN, Amir · MANNING, Michelle · MECHANIC, William M. · MELEDANDRI, Christopher · MEYER, Barry, and Alan Horn · MEYER, Ron · MULLIGAN, Brian C., and Stacey Snider · NATHANSON, Michael · ORDESKY, Mark · PASCAL, Amy · POSTER, Meryl · PULA, Chris · ROTH, Joe · ROTHMAN, Tom · SACKMAN, Jeff · SCHNEIDER, Peter · SHAYE, Robert · SHERAK, Tom · STRINGER, Howard · VITALE, Ruth, and David Dinerstein · WEINSTEIN, Bob · WEINSTEIN, Harvey · WIGAN, Gareth · YEMENIDJIAN, Alex, and Chris McGurk · ZISKIN, Laura

EXECS

Virtually all businesses can be broken down into buyers and sellers. In the film business, virtually everyone is selling something: Stars sell their acting talent and box-office appeal, managers and agents sell their clients' services or material, producers sell their projects. Studio production and acquisition execs are among the few real buyers in the industry, saying yes, no, and maybe on a daily basis to scripts, major casting decisions, and production starts.

Relatively few of today's executives have experience actually making movies, so their decisions are often seen as arbitrary by the legions of sellers hawking their wares on the studio lots. But studio execs, especially those at the very top with the power to greenlight a movie, must live or die by their choices.

While studio honchos typically enjoy seven-figure salaries and lavish perks, they are only at the periphery of the glow generated by a commercial or critical success. And a string of flops can mean an unceremonious and extremely public firing. While the usual studio golden parachute includes a production deal on the lot, many former honchos have found they're not necessarily cut out for the life of producer. After all, talented buyers don't always make good salesmen.

MICHAEL BARKER, TOM BERNARD, AND MARCIE BLOOM

Co-Presidents

Sony Pictures Classics

Michael Barker, Tom Bernard, and Marcie Bloom continue to run Sony Pictures Classics with the same diligence and soft-spoken aggressiveness that has kept them at the top of the independent heap since taking over the specialized banner in 1992. Though Bloom has been ill in the last year, Barker and Bernard, along with

MICHAEL BARKER, TOM BERNARD, AND MARCIE BLOOM (CON'T)

550 Madison Ave.
New York, NY 10022-3211
Phone: (212) 833-8833
Fax: (212) 833-8844

vice-president Dylan Leiner, have maintained the company's strategy of buying, then marketing and releasing films by acclaimed talent (like David Mamet and Mike Figgis) cheaply and effectively. Often, Sony Classics won't go higher than a few million in acquisition and domestic prints and advertising costs on any given film. But this hasn't hurt their bottom line, with success coming from such well-regarded titles as *Mi Vida Loca*, *Ma Vie en Rose*, *Welcome to the Dollhouse*, *Waiting for Guffman*, and *Vanya on 42nd St.* Among the films they've endeavored to finance on their own are *The Spanish Prisoner* and *The Winslow Boy*. Based in New York, Bernard and Barker are mainstays of the festival circuit (Cannes, Sundance, Toronto, Venice, Telluride, and London), where they often manage to snatch undiscovered gems out from under their competitors' noses.

JEFF BLAKE

President of Worldwide Sales and Distribution

Columbia Pictures
c/o Sony Pictures Releasing
10202 West Washington Blvd.
Culver City, CA 90232-3195
Phone: (310) 244-4000
Fax: (310) 244-2626

After getting his start programming for a college film society, Jeff Blake is one of the smartest—and certainly the wittiest—members of the elite club of studio distribution heads. Early in his career, unsure of his future in distribution, Blake put himself through law school at night and passed the bar. There is no question he would've made a good lawyer: Blake is known as a tough negotiator in his dealings with theater owners. As part of Sony's new Screen Gems team, he had a voice in deciding which completed films Sony acquired for domestic distribution.

In 1999, Sony rewarded Blake's five years of

outstanding performance with the title of worldwide president. This move brought the studio's international theatrical division, Columbia TriStar Film Distributors Intl., under his domain; its president, Duncan Clark, now reports to Blake. During his tenure, the studio had its best year ever in 1997, when it scored all-time industry records with a domestic theatrical gross of $1.27 billion.

JOHN CALLEY

Chairman

Sony Pictures Entertainment
10202 West Washington Blvd.
Thalberg Building
Culver City, CA 90232-3195
Phone: (310) 244-4000
Fax: (310) 244-2626

After a hiatus from the film business for more than a decade (becoming a gentleman farmer in Connecticut), in 1994 John Calley returned with a vengeance and recorded a string of stunning successes as head of United Artists. Using know-how he had developed as head of production at Warner Bros. from 1968 to 1981, Calley put together pics with old cronies like Mike Nichols (*The Birdcage*). The result led Sony Corp. President Nobuyuki Idei to beg Calley to come to Sony and make it well again. Sony had been through the wringer with a record $2.7 billion write-off in 1994, and morale had bottomed out. After Calley moved to Sony in 1996, he cleaned house of most of the executives from Peter Guber and Jon Peters's high-flying days atop the studio and enjoyed the fruits of the departing team with hits like *Men in Black*, *Air Force One*, and *My Best Friend's Wedding*. Now, close to retirement, Calley runs things on autopilot. He's already all but announced a successor in Columbia president Amy Pascal.

PETER CHERNIN

President/COO, News Corporation, and Chairman/CEO, Fox Group

c/o 20th Century Fox
10201 West Pico Blvd.
Building 100
Los Angeles, CA 90035
Phone: (310) 369-1000
Fax: (310) 369-3846

Criticized during the making of *Titanic* (a film he greenlighted when he was chairman of Fox Filmed Entertainment) for playing the executive equivalent of "Where's Waldo," Peter Chernin later took responsibility for the pic—albeit once it was on its way to its record-setting $1.8 billion box office. To his credit, despite being promoted to his NewsCorp post in 1996, Chernin often stepped in to try to mollify and manage James Cameron, the autocratic director of the $200-plus-million pic. Chernin, a onetime publicist, is respected for his business acumen and for the breadth of his responsibilities, which include overseeing all of NewsCorp's North American media operations (i.e., Fox Filmed Entertainment, Fox Television Studios, HarperCollins publishers, and the Los Angeles Dodgers). While Chernin is credited as a hands-off manager, he will step in occasionally to overrule even his top execs for the greater good of Rupert Murdoch's NewsCorp. This was the case with the high-profile event pic *Minority Report*, for which the studio negotiated a complex pay structure for director Steven Spielberg and star Tom Cruise, giving the duo as much as 45 percent of the film's eventual gross. While some execs balked at giving up so much of the studio's upside, Chernin saw the worldwide marketing cachet of the pairing, even if the studio doesn't make a dime on the film.

RICHARD COOK

Chairman

Dick Cook began working for Disney as a ride operator at Disneyland in 1970. Twenty-six years later he had climbed up the Disney corpo-

RICHARD COOK (CON'T)

Buena Vista
Motion Picture Group
500 South Buena Vista St.
Team Disney Building
Burbank, CA 91521
Phone: (818) 560-1000
Fax: (818) 841-3112

rate ladder through stints in pay-TV, theatrical sales, and finally distribution and marketing, ultimately landing as chairman of the Motion Picture Group. That last bump in 1996, which made him number two in the Disney food chain, came only after upstart DreamWorks tried to woo him away. Cook has been responsible for staging such events as the launch of *Pocahontas* in New York's Central Park and the Mardi Gras-like premiere of *Hunchback of Notre Dame* in New Orleans. He also championed the company's refurbishment of the El Capitan Theater in L.A., which is now used to screen all the major Disney animation ventures. As an executive, he is held in high esteem for his experience in all areas of the Mouse House, but Cook is seen as posing little threat to either Disney chairman Michael Eisner or Disney Studios chairman Joe Roth.

ROBERT A. DALY AND TERRY SEMEL

Former Co-Chairmen/Co-CEOs

Warner Bros. &
Warner Music Group
4000 Warner Blvd.
Building 2
Burbank, CA 91522
Phone: (818) 954-6000
Fax: (818) 954-3232

In a move that jolted Hollywood awake from its summer slumber, in July 1999, Warner Bros. co-chiefs Bob Daly and Terry Semel announced their resignations from the studio they had headed for almost twenty years. The execs, who both held the rank of chairman and co-CEO of the Warner studio and Warner Music Group, informed Time Warner chairman Gerald Levin in a letter that they had decided "not to pursue new employment contracts with Time Warner when [the] current ones expire at the end of the year." The two said they had been mulling over the "extremely difficult decision" for some time. In a subsequent statement, they explained, "For some months now, we have been giving careful thought to the possibility of pursuing new challenges and opportunities." Whatever really happened, the duo's departure from the Burbank lot marks the end of an era—one characterized by high-octane film franchises, star-producing deals, and legendary perks such as private dining rooms and corporate jets. Daly and Semel were trained at the knee of legendary Time Warner chairman Steve Ross, and their lavish operating style always reflected Ross's generosity to his senior executives and top talent. In a Hollywood fraught with continual studio upheaval—not to mention frequent ownership changes—Daly and Semel were a constant. And their strong batting average at the box office earned them the respect of both Wall Street and their competitors. During their tenure, Warner Bros. evolved from a traditional movie distribution company, with revenues of $670 million in 1980, to the $10 billion film, television, and music congolmerate of today. Its numerous hugely successful pics during the period included *Batman, Twister,* the *Lethal Weapon* series as well as *The Fugitive.*

MICHAEL DE LUCA

President

New Line Cinema

116 North Robertson Blvd.

Second Floor

Los Angeles, CA 90048

Mike De Luca is a strange mixture of old and new Hollywood. With a deadly eye for what makes successful films, he has been chased by virtually every studio in town. Ever the Brooklyn boy, he stays with New Line because he has absolute autonomy to pick the films he likes and makes them with people he enjoys. De Luca has personally overseen New Line's transformation

MICHAEL DE LUCA (CON'T)

Phone: (310) 854-5811

Fax: (310) 854-1824

from horrormeister (*Nightmare on Elm Street*) to major distributor and producer of box office gold like *Seven*, *Dumb and Dumber*, *The Mask*, *The Wedding Singer*, *Austin Powers: International Man of Mystery*, and *Austin Powers: The Spy Who Shagged Me*. He also has taken chances with films that simply intrigued him, like *Boogie Nights* and *American History X*. De Luca has long cultivated a "bad boy" image in Hollywood with everything from acknowledged drug use to fistfights at upscale eatery Mr. Chow's to oral sex on the lawn at William Morris Agency topper Arnold Rifkin's 1998 Oscar party. Bottom line for him, though, is that he's loyal to New Line chairman Bob Shaye, who serves as a persevering father figure to the wild one.

LORENZO DI BONAVENTURA

President of Production

Warner Bros. Pictures

4000 Warner Blvd.

Building 3

Burbank, CA 91522

Phone: (818) 954-6000

Fax: (818) 954-2870

Lorenzo di Bonaventura looked to be ushered out the door in early 1998 when Warner suffered such flops as *Midnight in the Garden of Good and Evil*, *Father's Day*, *The Postman*, *Sphere*, and *Mad City*. At the time, he shared the president of production post with Billy Gerber. After Warner demoted Gerber to a production deal and gave Di Bonaventura a solo shot at the job, industry pundits still had him crashing and burning. To his credit, Di Bonaventura persevered and was partially responsible for a Warner comeback with hits like *The Matrix* and *Analyze This*. Whether he will stay is anyone's guess. The executive has had interest from other studios. His former bosses, Bob Daly and Terry Semel, seem to like him; but of course, they also seemed to like Bruce Berman, whom he and Gerber first replaced in 1996. Now he must convince a new regime that he's the man for the job. One of Hollywood's keenest minds, Di Bonaventura is coming into his own with overall game plans for the studio.

JONATHAN DOLGEN
Chairman
Viacom Entertainment Group
c/o Paramount Pictures
5555 Melrose Ave.
Administration Building
Room 200
Los Angeles, CA 90038
Phone: (323) 956-5000

Dolgen is the force behind Paramount's once maligned and now widely imitated policy of seeking co-financing partners on virtually every feature production. That conservative policy has yielded the studio roughly half the take on such hits as *Saving Private Ryan*, *Deep Impact*, and a little thing called *Titanic*. Known for a caustic wit, the former attorney doesn't hand out praise easily, a cause for some grousing among Par execs. Still, Paramount has enjoyed little turnover in its upper ranks since Dolgen's arrival from Sony in 1994. On his own time, Dolgen is a passionate and eclectic music fan who once asked that Bob Dylan perform at a charity dinner honoring the studio topper—a request Dylan granted.

DAN FELLMAN
President
Warner Bros. Distribution
Theatrical Distribution

Fellman, who for two decades served as second in command to Barry Reardon, finally ascended to Warner Bros.' top distribution spot in 1999. It's a given that he has big shoes to fill in replacing the astute and charismatic Reardon, long considered by his peers to be the "dean of distri-

DAN FELLMAN (CON'T)

4000 Warner Blvd.
Building 154
Room 2111
Burbank, CA 91522
Phone: (818) 954-6000
Fax: (818) 954-3927

bution." But though Warners suffered a dry spell in the years leading up to Fellman's ascent, the venerable—and prolific—studio still has clout with exhibitors, who know they can count on WB to provide a steady flow of product and at least a couple of blockbusters a year. Fellman started his career as a sales exec at Paramount in 1965, but like many distribution honchos, he did a stint as an exhibitor, first with Loews Theatres and later forming his own company. He joined Warner Bros. in 1978—just a month after Reardon—and for over twenty years oversaw the day-to-day operations of the studio's domestic theatrical distribution division.

LUCY FISHER

Vice Chairman

Columbia TriStar Motion Picture Group, Sony Pictures Entertainment
10202 West Washington Blvd.
Thalberg Building
Culver City, CA 90232
Phone: (310) 244-4000
Fax: (310) 244-2626

A cum laude grad of Harvard, Lucy Fisher has always lurched upward in Hollywood through executive positions at 20th Century Fox, Francis Ford Coppola's American Zoetrope, Warner Bros., and finally Sony Pictures Entertainment. At Warner, she developed a reputation for having great relationships with directors Steven Spielberg, George Miller, Spike Lee, and Clint Eastwood. She also drew gibes for, heaven forbid, working less than sixty hours a week so that she could raise her three kids. At Sony, she has sown some of those early relationships, such as Steven Spielberg for *Memoirs of a Geisha*. She also works closely with John Calley, Gareth Wigan, and Amy Pascal as Sony's Four Musketeers of production. Her husband, Doug Wick, is firmly ensconced as a producer on the Sony lot, where he has produced such films as *Wolf*.

ROB FRIEDMAN

Vice Chairman
Paramount Motion Pictures Group
c/o Paramount Pictures
5555 Melrose Ave.
Dressing Room Building
Suite 100
Los Angeles, CA 90038
Phone: (323) 956-5000
Fax: (323) 862-2220

Friedman replaced Barry London as Paramount vice-chairman in 1996 after spending more than a quarter-century as Warner Bros.' marketing chief and corporate spokesperson. At Par, Friedman oversees all aspects of marketing and distribution, though marketing is still his forte. Known as a hands-on exec—too hands-on for some—Friedman has overseen campaigns for such high-profile Par hits as *Titanic*, *The Truman Show*, and *Deep Impact*. But the tight-lipped, that's-our-story-and-we're-sticking-to-it approach to publicity that served him well as corporate flack for WB has sometimes made him seem positively out of the loop among his more media-savvy Melrose Ave. colleagues.

TODD GARNER AND NINA JACOBSON

Co-Presidents
Buena Vista Motion Picture Group
500 South Buena Vista St.
Team Disney Building
Burbank, CA 91521
Phone: (818) 560-1000
Fax(es):
Garner—(818) 560-4009
Jacobson—(818) 562-6920

In May 1999 Todd Garner and Nina Jacobson were upped from their executive vice-presidents' posts to co-presidents of the Buena Vista Motion Picture Group, the umbrella over Walt Disney Studios' live action feature activities. Taking over the duties formerly handled by David Vogel, who left after losing an internal power struggle with Walt Disney Studios prexy Peter Schneider, the newly installed duo was charged with overseeing development and production chores for films produced under all three Buena Vista labels (Walt Disney, Touchstone, and Hollywood Pictures). Though the reporting structure was never spelled out, it was tacitly understood that Garner would continue to focus mainly on Touchstone films and report to Walt Disney chairman Joe Roth, while

Jacobson would continue to work mainly on Walt Disney films, for which she would report to Schneider, and some Touchstone or Hollywood projects, reporting to Roth in those cases. Garner started with Touchstone Pictures in 1990 as a creative exec, and while moving up the company ladder he has worked on such pics as *The Waterboy*, *Con Air*, and *Father of the Bride*. Jacobson joined Walt Disney Pictures/Hollywood Pictures from DreamWorks in 1998 as exec VP of production. Since then, she has overseen such pics as Hollywood Pictures' *The Sixth Sense* and *Mission to Mars*.

MARK GILL

President

Miramax/L.A.

7966 Beverly Blvd.

Los Angeles, CA 90048

Phone: (323) 951-4200

Fax: (323) 951-4215

A politically savvy exec, Mark Gill is generally respected and well liked by those who have worked with him. Miramax co-chair Harvey Weinstein has described him as "the smartest marketing executive in the business." Since joining Miramax in 1994, Gill has overseen marketing campaigns for such films as *Pulp Fiction*, *Scream*, *Il Postino*, *The English Patient*, and *Shakespeare in Love*. A former reporter for *Newsweek* and the *L.A. Times* and later a publicist, Gill did a six-year stint as a marketing exec at Sony before moving to the New York–based mini-major. In 1997, he was in talks to join fledgling PolyGram Films, in large part because of his desire to return to his native L.A. It was then that Miramax toppers Harvey and Bob Weinstein made Gill an offer he couldn't refuse by creating the new post of president Miramax/L.A. As an additional measure of Gill's key role at the company, his contract included a clause stipulating that Gill could put his young family first—even before the notoriously demanding Freres Weinstein.

SCOTT GREENSTEIN

Chairman

RUSSELL SCHWARTZ

President

USA Films

65 Bleecker Street

Second Floor

New York, NY 10012

Phone: (212) 539-4000

Fax: Greenstein—

(212) 539-4099

When Barry Diller bought specialized distributor October Films and niche mini-studio Gramercy Pictures from Universal in the spring of 1999, and combined them to form USA Films, few industryites believed he could get Gramercy topper Russell Schwartz and October's Scott Greenstein to run the new production and distribution entity together. The soft-spoken Schwartz is known for his taste and marketing acumen both as head of Gramercy, where he released *Four Weddings and a Funeral*, *Dead Man Walking*, and *Fargo*, and as exec VP at Miramax in the late '80s and early '90s (*Cinema Paradiso*, *My Left Foot*). Greenstein, who replaced Amir Malin as one of October's three co-presidents shortly after October was acquired by Universal in 1997, is known as a gruff, gloves-off competitor and a fierce negotiator in the style of his former mentors, Miramax co-chairmen Bob and Harvey Weinstein. Greenstein spent four years at the mini-major, where he served as senior VP of motion pictures, music, new media, and publishing. While their areas of expertise are a good fit, Greenstein and Schwartz's personalities and styles are different enough that some wonder how long the marriage will last, especially under Diller, who is known to trade in top executives the way some people trade in cars.

ROBERT HARPER

President of Worldwide Marketing
Fox Filmed Entertainment
10201 West Pico Blvd.
Building 88
Los Angeles, CA 90035
Phone: (310) 369-1000
Fax: (310) 369-2105

Robert Harper, who had been president of marketing for Fox, was rewarded for his work on such films as *Independence Day*, *William Shakespeare's Romeo + Juliet,* and *Soul Food* with the title of worldwide marketing president in 1998. The promotion also served to keep the highly respected marketing maven within the Fox fold after a couple of suitors came calling. Harper oversees marketing for all areas of Fox Filmed Entertainment, which includes theatrical, home entertainment, licensing and merchandising, and music divisions. Harper, who enjoys more creative and administrative participation than most of his marketing counterparts, has emerged as one of the industry's premier marketing mavens, separating himself from most of his contemporaries by his ability to move flexibly and effectively from the biggest of event pics (think *ID4*) to R-rated, offbeat comedies like *There's Something About Mary* to targeted female pics like *Ever After*. Since he joined Fox in 1985, Harper has worked in numerous areas of the company, including the advertising and production arms. He served his first stint as head of marketing in 1989, a job he held for 18 months before inking a first-look producing deal with Fox, where he produced the 1993 film *Rookie of the Year*. He rejoined the exec ranks in 1995, when he again was named president of marketing.

SHERRY LANSING

Chairman

The producer of both commercial pics (*Indecent Proposal*) and acclaimed ones (*The Accused*), Lansing commands the respect of filmmakers as

SHERRY LANSING (CON'T)

Paramount Motion Picture Group
c/o Paramount Pictures
5555 Melrose Ave.
Administration Building
Room 100
Los Angeles, CA 90038
Phone: (323) 956-5000
Fax: (323) 862-8510

a studio chief who has actually made movies. Charming and likable, she can also be tough as nails when it comes to getting what she wants. Conservative by nature—she reportedly keeps much of her personal portfolio in T-bills—before greenlighting a pic of any sizable budget, Lansing likes to have insurance in the form of bankable—but preferably not too expensive—stars.

She was criticized for refusing to pay Will Smith $12 million, just before his quote jumped to $20 million. But Lansing has had the last laugh: between Paramount's co-financing policy, its thrifty MTV and Nickelodeon pics, and its penchant for successful mid-range comedies and dramas, Lansing can actually point to bottom-line figures written in black ink.

LINDSAY LAW

President

Fox Searchlight Pictures
10201 West Pico Blvd.
Building 38
Los Angeles, CA 90035
Phone: (310) 369-1000
Fax: (310) 369-2359

Lindsay Law, the former president and CEO of New York–based Playhouse Intl., joined Searchlight in 1995 after the specialized banner's founder and first prexy, Tom Rothman, was promoted to head the 20th Century Fox division. Law is a veteran independent film producer who has navigated between the rarefied world of public broadcasting and the Hollywood creative community for nearly two decades. During his fourteen years at American Playhouse, Law oversaw more than forty productions, including critical faves like Norman Rene's *Longtime Companion*, Matty Rich's *Straight Out of Brooklyn*, and Errol Morris's *The Thin Blue Line*. At Searchlight, Law has experienced the thrill of the enormous worldwide hit, *The Full Monty*, coupled with the agony of such box office duds as *Cousin Bette*, *Polish Wedding*, and *The Slums of Beverly Hills*. But the $246 million worldwide gross of *Full Monty* in 1997 didn't just keep the label in business; the $3 million pic, although largely an anomaly, showed the art-house world the potential of a well-crafted, low-budget movie.

ROBERT LEVIN

Chairman of Worldwide Marketing

Sony Pictures Entertainment
10202 West Washington Blvd.
TriStar Building
Culver City, CA 90232
Phone: (310) 244-4000
Fax: (310) 244-2626

Bob Levin is often considered a quiet, carry-a-big-stick kind of guy. He has, without public fanfare, turned Sony into a feature powerhouse, overseeing all films en route to Sony's marketing on the $1 billion–plus year in domestic gross of 1997. Now, he's been elevated to a lofty post that meanders between Sony's Tokyo headquarters and the Sony Pictures California lot. The company recently started the Screen Gems label for him to oversee as a side duty. Levin made it clear that the label would be market driven with little or no development, only production and acquisition of films. He spends much time jetting around the world to coalesce the approach for Sony as a corporation. Levin had been with Disney for more than ten years before moving to Savoy Pictures, which closed unceremoniously in 1995.

WAYNE LEWELLEN

President Domestic Distribution

A larger-than-life Texas native who doesn't suffer fools gladly, Lewellen has held the reins of Paramount's domestic distribution efforts since 1984, adding international oversight in 1993. A twenty-five-year Par veteran, Lewellen is known

WAYNE LEWELLEN (CON'T)

Paramount Pictures
5555 Melrose Ave.
Los Angeles, CA 90038
Phone: (323) 956-5000
Fax: (323) 862-1477

as a fierce negotiator with a long memory. After AMC crossed Lewellen over the booking of *The Firm* in 1993, the ensuing cold war cost AMC big time five years later when Par released *Titanic*. While he answers to Par vice-chairman Rob Friedman, Lewellen has a long-standing close relationship with Viacom chairman Sumner Redstone, an exhibition veteran who takes an active interest in distribution issues, including release dates.

MICHAEL LYNNE

President/COO

New Line Cinema
888 Seventh Avenue
20th Floor
New York, NY 10106
Phone: (212) 649-4900
Fax: (212) 649-4966

Michael Lynne gads about Gotham with the reckless abandon of a chief operating officer of a film company who also has a house in the Hamptons. If he's not in his office, he's usually at Elaine's, waiting for box-office results. Lynne was a law school pal of New Line chief Bob Shaye's long before the studio was hatched in 1967. Lynne was brought in early by Shaye to help set the company in motion, and his business acumen has been one of the primary reasons that New Line has succeeded at navigating the treacherous waters between niche genre films like *Nightmare on Elm Street* and big-ticket items like *Lost in Space*. When the rumor surfaced that Shaye and Lynne might be elevated within the Time Warner fold to take over Warner Bros. from Bob Daly and Terry Semel, a lot of industry types thought Lynne was responsible for floating his own trial balloon.

LAURIE MACDONALD AND WALTER PARKES

Co-Heads of Production

c/o DreamWorks SKG
100 Universal City Plaza
Building 10
Universal City, CA 91608
Phone: (818) 733-7000
Fax: (818) 733-9996

The husband-and-wife team that took over Spielberg's Amblin Entertainment in 1993 (a year after husband-and-wife team Kathleen Kennedy and Frank Marshall ankled) now occupies a unique position at DreamWorks Pictures. The pair divides their time and attention among three areas: working closely with Spielberg to develop and produce projects he directs, developing other projects that they produce themselves, and overseeing DreamWorks' live-action production efforts. They shared the latter responsibility with former Dream Works production chief Robert Cooper until his ouster in the summer of 1999. During the final Amblin years, the pair served as producers or exec producers on an amazing quartet of blockbusters that were all released in less than a year: *The Lost World: Jurassic Park*, *Men in Black*, *Twister*, and *The Mask of Zorro*. The levelheaded couple met on the James Woods courtroom drama *True Believer*: She was the studio exec, he was the producer. Parkes, himself an accomplished screenwriter, gets high marks from filmmakers for his story acumen, and both are known for bringing out the best in creative types.

AMIR MALIN

Co-President

Artisan Entertainment

Amir Malin has gone from exec producer on such indie films as *Scenes from the Class Struggle in Beverly Hills*, *Swimming to Cambodia*, *Matewan*, and *Miles from Home*, to running, as a partner, the fast-growing production/distribution banner, Artisan Entertainment. In between, he was a partner in October Films before it was sold to Universal in 1997. In his current post, Malin has helped trans-

AMIR MALIN (CON'T)
157 Chambers St.
12th Floor
New York, NY 10007
Phone: (212) 577-2400
Fax: (212) 577-2890

form the former Live Entertainment, a foundering video label with underutilized assets, into a potent moneymaker with a library of more than six thousand film titles. Malin knows how to exploit those titles for profit, with more than $7 million a month showing up on the Artisan bottom line from the video sales alone. Though Malin runs Artisan with Bill Block and Mark Curcio, he is the frontman for that company. Known as a shrewd businessman, Malin, who tends to parcel out the truth economically, is working to build Artisan as a force in the business and one that will be attractive to potential suitors, particularly new media companies looking for "content."

MICHELLE MANNING

President of Production
c/o Paramount Pictures
5555 Melrose Ave.
Administration Building
Room 243
Los Angeles, CA 90038
Phone: (323) 956-5000
Fax: (323) 862-0388

Known as a filmmaker-friendly exec with a keen eye for material, Manning is one of the few production honchos with extensive experience in both physical and creative production. She's even directed film (*Blue City*) and TV (*Miami Vice*). After getting her start as a production supervisor for Francis Ford Coppola, Manning joined Ned Tanen's Channel Prods., where she produced John Hughes's 1980s teen classics *The Breakfast Club* and *Sixteen Candles*. After an exec stint at Orion Pictures, she moved to Par as a senior VP in 1991. There she oversaw such hits as *The Firm*, *Clueless*, and *Forrest Gump*, before moving into the president post in 1997. In addition to her own considerable talents, Manning has an ace in the hole at Par: her close relationship with the tempestuous and prolific Scott Rudin, easily the studio's most effective producer.

WILLIAM M. MECHANIC

Chairman/CEO

Fox Filmed Entertainment
10201 West Pico Blvd.
Building 88
Los Angeles, CA 90035
Phone: (310) 369-1000
Fax: (310) 369-2105

As chairman and CEO of Fox Filmed Entertainment, Bill Mechanic is the force behind all the studio's worldwide operations, including production, marketing, and distribution as well as all video, interactive, licensing and merchandising, and music. Since taking the reins of the studio in 1996 after Peter Chernin was promoted to a NewsCorp. post, Mechanic has put his imprimatur on a diverse slate of films that have experienced varying degrees of commercial and critical success, including *The Thin Red Line*, *There's Something About Mary*, *Titanic*, *William Shakespeare's Romeo+Juliet*, *Dr. Dolittle*, *The Fight Club*, *Alien Resurrection*, *Soul Food*, and *Anastasia*. Mechanic is that true Hollywood rarity: a man of conviction. The Detroit native is regarded as a tough negotiator who can, and does, say no to coddled stars and directors, but he does not play games. At times laconic and downright grumpy, Mechanic—who has survived such eight-hundred-pound auteur gorillas as James Cameron, George Lucas, and Warren Beatty—is roundly admired for his straightforward management style, which commands the respect of his underlings and those outside the studio. Beginning with the holiday 1999 releases and continuing through 2000, Mechanic has put together the most envied slate of films in Hollywood, including the *The Beach*, starring Leonardo DiCaprio under Danny Boyle's helm; *Anna*, the Jodie Foster, Chow Yun-Fat take on *The King and I*; the Steven Spielberg–Tom Cruise sci-fi thriller *Minority Report*; Baz Luhrmann's *Moulin Rouge*, starring Ewan McGregor and Nicole Kidman; and *Me, Myself and Irene*, starring Jim Carrey for the Farrelly brothers.

CHRISTOPHER MELEDANDRI

President

Fox Animation Studios
10201 West Pico Blvd.
Building 58
Los Angeles, CA 90035
Phone: (310) 369-1000
Fax: (310) 369-3907

As prexy of Fox Animation Studios, Chris Meledandri oversees all animated, stop-motion, mixed-media, and digitally produced feature films for the Fox Filmed Entertainment banner. Originally dubbed Fox Family Films, the division was renamed and reconstituted in its present FAS form in early 1998, following the successful, $127 million grossing, release of the studio's first animated feature, *Anastasia*. Consequently, the division—which had produced live actioners such as *Mighty Morphin Power Rangers: The Movie* as well as its sequel, *Dunston Checks In*, and *Home Alone 3*—cut back on its live-action offerings in order to concentrate on animated fare, but not before finishing and releasing the Drew Barrymore–starring hit *Ever After*. With Fox brass pulling for him (and fully committed to taking Disney on in the animated arena), Meledandri has overseen Fox's second animated feature, *Titan A.E.* (formerly titled *Planet Ice*), which is expected to be the animated event for summer 2000. And in mid-1999, he began production on the combination live-action and stop-motion animation pic *Monkeybone*, starring Brendan Fraser and Whoopi Goldberg. As part of his duties, the former producer oversees the 66,000-square-foot Fox Animation Studios in Phoenix, which is equipped to produce all forms of animated, stop-motion, mixed-media, and digitally produced feature films.

BARRY MEYER AND ALAN HORN

A few weeks after Robert Daly and Terry Semel announced their surprise resignations from the

BARRY MEYER AND ALAN HORN (CON'T)
Chairman/CEO and President/COO
Warner Bros.
400 Warner Blvd.
Burbank, CA 91522
Phone: (818) 954-6000
Fax: (818) 954-3232

top posts at Warner Bros. studio and music, veteran Time Warner exec Barry Meyer was chosen to run the works as chairman and CEO of Warner Bros., with former Castle Rock Entertainment head Alan Horn named as second-in-command. The two are emphasizing stability and continuity at the studio. They were scheduled to start officially on October 4. The move by Time Warner ended weeks of intense speculation over the succession at the studio.

Meyer had served most recently as Warner Bros. chief operating officer. Horn, who was chairman and CEO of Castle Rock Entertainment, the mini-studio Time Warner acquired in 1996 through its purchase of Turner Broadcasting, became Warner Bros. president and chief operating officer. The appointments of Meyer and Horn marks the entry of bottom-liners into the venerable studio. Under the new regime, a different Warners hopes to emerge as a nimble, but also cautious and cost-conscious studio. Meyer, who has worked at WB since 1971, had been the studio's exec VP and chief operating officer. A trained lawyer and company insider, he has earned plaudits as the head of WB's TV division—the biggest profit center in the organization. Horn, who was considered a dark horse in the leadership race, is close to Time Warner vice chairman Ted Turner and has a solid background in business administration and film financing. A Harvard Business School graduate, he is well-liked in Hollywood. Under the new structure, Meyer runs the studio, reporting to Levin through Time Warner president Richard Parsons. Warners's home-video and consumer product divisions report directly to Meyer. Horn, who reports to Meyer, oversees theatrical production, distribution, and marketing.

RON MEYER

President/COO

Universal Studios
100 Universal City Plaza
Building LRW
14th Floor
Universal City, CA 91608
Phone: (818) 777-1000
Fax: (818) 777-2500

Ron Meyer's marine training, 1962–64, may have been the most useful education he ever had as far as Hollywood goes. So creating CAA, a major Hollywood talent agency, with Mike Ovitz and three other William Morris Agency defectors in 1975 was cake. As the agency quickly grew to include such superstars of the time as Kevin Costner, Sylvester Stallone, Michael Jackson, David Letterman, Sydney Pollack, Madonna, Robin Williams, Michael Crichton, and Jonathan Demme, Meyer was considered the well-liked "mollifier" for the fast-rising percentery. After Ovitz negotiated himself out of Universal Studios' invitation to run the company, Universal turned to Meyer. He started back in 1995 and has watched Universal become a shell of its former self under Seagram scion Edgar Bronfman, Jr. He's been termed the "Teflon executive" because while Universal has burned, he's been allowed to fiddle. And when no one wanted the top film post after Casey Silver was axed, Meyer stepped up again, saying he would simply get up a little earlier each day to handle the workload. If Universal can survive its current filmic mess, Meyer will likely continue collecting a paycheck. That is, if Bronfman maintains Universal's feature interest at all.

BRIAN C. MULLIGAN AND STACEY SNIDER

Co-chairmen

KEVIN MISHER

President of Production

Universal Pictures
100 Universal City Plaza
Building 488
Eighth Floor
Universal City, CA 91608
Phone: (818) 777-1000
Fax(es):
Mulligan—(818) 866-5069
Snider—(818) 866-2151

In June 1999, Universal Studios promoted Brian C. Mulligan and Stacey Snider to co-chairmen of Universal Pictures. Snider now oversees all feature film production, marking and domestic distribution while Mulligan is responsible for finance, business affairs, legal, human resources, administration, international operations, and home video. The duo both hold greenlighting authority, although Universal Studios president and chief operating officer Ron Meyer has final say on what goes before the cameras. Snider, who has been president of production since November 1998, joined Universal in 1996, when she and former co-president of production Marc Platt left TriStar Pictures to run production at Universal. With the promotion, Snider solidifies her position as one of the most powerful women in Hollywood, joining Paramount Motion Picture Group's Sherry Lansing as the only female chairs of major studios. Mulligan, an eight-year Universal veteran, had served as executive vice president of operations and finance. In his exec posts at U, Mulligan has been involved in negotiating the studio's $1.1 billion film financing agreement with Citibank; and the acquisition of USA Networks and the subsequent merger of U's television assets with Barry Diller's USA Networks. The new setup already has started to pay off for the motion picture group. Despite a string of disappointing films in 1998 and early 1999—including *Virus, EDtv, Meet Joe Black,* and *Babe: Pig in the City*—the strategy of bolstering international production and distribution has led to strong overseas B.O. recently. U's recent hits include *The Mummy* (which has grossed more than $300 million worldwide), and Working Title's *Notting Hill* and *American Pie*. In August 1999, Universal upped Kevin Misher, who had served as co-president of production since November 1998, to president of production. Misher now has the full support of his superiors, and with the unshared title, he oversees all feature film production, reporting directly to Snider and Mulligan. Misher came to U after six years as a production exec at TriStar Pictures, rising to senior vice president in 1993.

MICHAEL NATHANSON

President

MGM Pictures

c/o Metro-Goldwyn-Mayer
2500 Broadway
Building F
Fifth Floor
Santa Monica, CA 90404-3061
Phone: (310) 449-3632
Fax: (310) 449-3632

While there has been widespread speculation that Michael Nathanson would be let go by MGM's latest changeover of corporate brass (Alex Yemenidjian and Chris McGurk) that occurred in April 1999, as of mid-1999, Nathanson was still in place. While ensconced at the most beleaguered studio in Hollywood, Nathanson continue to go about daily chores, trying to put together competitive film slates for a studio whose ownership commitment and economic viability are always being questioned. Among the obstacles he faced were wary agents, unwilling to send their best material to the studio or to place their top talent in its films—unless MGM/UA is willing to overpay, as has been the case recently. During his tenure, Nathanson has witnessed one failure after another, including *Disturbing Behavior*, *Species 2*, *At First Sight*, and *The Mod Squad*. But Nathanson is known as a survivor and an adept political player, so if he doesn't remain in place at MGM, he will likely land on his feet at another studio or production company. Nathanson joined MGM in 1997 from New Regency Prods., where he was chairman and CEO, overseeing such pics as *L.A. Confidential*, *A Time to Kill*, *Tin Cup*, and *Heat*.

MARK ORDESKY

President

Fine Line Features
116 North Robertson Blvd.
Suite 509
Los Angeles, CA 90048
Phone: (310) 854-5811
Fax: (310) 854-1824

Mark Ordesky has been through the mill to reach the top of the indie heap at Fine Line Features. A longtime acquisitions maven for parent company New Line Cinema, Ordesky practically inherited the job through attrition of other executives (Ira Deutchman, Ruth Vitale, and Jonathan Weisgal) over the last five years. Ordesky, however, is close to New Line chairman Bob Shaye and runs the company with an eye toward the bottom line, which is not something his predecessors seemed intent on doing. Already, he's dressing in suits rather than the traditional New Line uniform of jeans and T-shirts. The company is charged with producing and acquiring low-budget, specialized offerings like Julio Medem's *Lovers of the Arctic Circle* and Anthony Drazan's *Hurlyburly*. If anything, Ordesky needs to develop stronger relationships with talent, but that, too, is coming as he puts together projects with Sean Penn, Kevin Spacey and Cameron Diaz.

AMY PASCAL

President

Amy Pascal is clearly one of Hollywood's premier executives, and lucky enough to work at a studio that professes to love her to the ends of the earth. Though she keeps moving upward, her track record has been lukewarm at best. When

AMY PASCAL (CON'T)
Columbia Pictures
10202 West Washington Blvd.
Thalberg Building
Culver City, CA 90232
Phone: (310) 244-4000
Fax: (310) 244-6161

she was running Turner Pictures, she set up several films that went on to decent box office results (namely, *You've Got Mail*, *City of Angels*); but her Columbia experience has been mostly a string of second-rate (but profitable) low-budget teen movies (*Can't Hardly Wait*, *Urban Legend*, and *Idle Hands*). Still, chairman John Calley has already dubbed her as his replacement at the top of Sony. Pascal has always been thought of as a first-tier story executive, and most consider her great with a script and writers (she spearheaded Sony's controversial deal giving writers 2 percent of a film's gross). But shifting into more global reasoning for product and marketing has been her most problematic challenge at Sony. In 1997, she married *New York Times* reporter Bernie Weinraub, which led to dozens of articles about the conflict of interest he faced in covering Hollywood for the *Times*. Two years later, the *Times* yanked him right out of Hollywood coverage and Pascal did not shy from voicing her displeasure.

MERYL POSTER

Co-President of Production
Miramax Films
Tribeca Film Center
375 Greenwich St.
New York, NY 10013
Phone: (212) 941-3800
Fax: (212) 941-2423

Poster began her film career in the prototypical Hollywood way: as an employee in the William Morris Agency's legendary mailroom. But it was her tenure as executive assistant to Gotham-based movie mogul Harvey Weinstein that started her on the path to running Miramax's production activities, along with former Turner Pictures exec Robert Osher. Poster juggles as many as sixty projects in production or development at a time, while Osher oversees physical production and business and legal affairs. As

Harvey turns his attention to the Disney subsid's expansion into TV, books, magazines, and other media, he has come to rely increasingly on Poster's judgment about film projects.

CHRIS PULA

President of Theatrical Marketing

Buena Vista Pictures Marketing

500 South Buena Vista St.

ROD Building

Burbank, CA 91521

Phone: (818) 560-1000

Fax: (818) 560-1999

Chris Pula came to Disney after a disastrous stint at Warner Bros. as head of marketing. His flamboyant, press-friendly style didn't mesh with the button-down, corporate sensibility of Warner co-chairs Terry Semel and Bob Daly. Pula, however, wasn't deterred. He thought about a number of options, not the least of which was retiring from the business altogether. But Disney chairman Joe Roth, who had been his boss at 20th Century Fox in the early 1990s, made him an outrageously lucrative offer to come to Disney, which was having problems with then head of marketing, John Cywinski. Outspoken and adamant about running his division his way, Pula was marketing films for New Line Cinema for several years before Warner Bros. He's got his hands full as Disney reduces the number of films it makes, increasing the pressure on those it does make to succeed. The only major drawback he's faced at Disney so far is the loss of publicity chief Terry Curtin, who opted out to go to Universal.

JOE ROTH

Chairman

Outside of Disney topper Michael Eisner, Joe Roth is the closest thing to a Lion King at the studio. The executive is in charge of all of the studio's feature film and TV ventures. But as he

JOE ROTH (CON'T)
Walt Disney Studios
500 South Buena Vista St.
Team Disney Building
Burbank, CA 91521
Phone: (818) 560-1000
Fax: (818) 566-4040

vacillates over whether to renew his contract, it's never clear if he even wants the job. Every time he starts to think about something else to do, Eisner offers him a bigger slice of the pie. For Roth, who has been a producer (helping establish the Morgan Creek and Caravan Pictures banners), director (*Streets of Gold*, *Revenge of the Nerds II: Nerds in Paradise*, and *Coupe de Ville*), and executive at 20th Century Fox and Disney, those slices seem to serve as little enticement to stay. When he went to Fox to take over, he was the first director to assume executive leadership since Ernst Lubitsch took over Paramount in 1935. As Disney seems to be in managerial flux at all times, Roth's job is uncertain only because he's uncertain whether he wants to be a suit, a creative type, or the coach of his kids' soccer teams. For the time being, however, it seems he'll stay the course.

TOM ROTHMAN

President of
Worldwide Production
20th Century Fox
10201 West Pico Blvd.
Building 88
Los Angeles, CA 90035
Phone: (310) 369-1000
Fax: (310) 369-1027

A former Gotham-based entertainment attorney, who represented independent filmmakers before coming to Hollywood in the mid-'80s, Rothman has used his indie experience to aid his way up the Hollywood food chain. In 1994, Fox tapped Rothman to launch the company's specialized banner, Fox Searchlight Pictures, which he christened with such pics as Edward Burns's *The Brothers McMullen*. Although Rothman was not an obvious choice to lead a mainstream production arm that releases a dozen pictures a year, in 1995, Fox once again turned to him to lead its flagship division, 20th Century Fox. While Chairman Bill Mechanic controls the green light at the studio, Rothman, who is described as both manic and brilliant, oversees development and production on all 20th pics. Among the films released under his watch have been *William Shakespeare's Romeo+Juliet*, *Independence Day*, *There's Something About Mary*, *Dr. Dolittle*, and the record-breaking, but wildly over budget, *Titanic* and the $150 million disaster *Speed 2*. Rothman's future looks pretty secure, since the exec has an incredibly strong slate for 2000, which includes Steven Spielberg's *Minority Report*, starring Tom Cruise; Danny Boyle's *The Beach*, starring Leonardo DiCaprio; the Farrelly bros.' *Me, Myself and Irene*, toplined by Jim Carrey, and the Bryan Singer–helmed *X-Men*, based on the Marvel Comics franchise.

JEFF SACKMAN

President

Lions Gate Films Corp.
2 Bloor St. West
Suite 1901
Toronto, Ontario, CA
M4W 3E2
Phone: (416) 944-0104
Fax: (416) 944-2212

Lions Gate Entertainment, the multifaceted film and TV production and distribution umbrella created in the late '90s by former investment banker and part-time producer Frank Giustra, is best known in the U.S. by its specialized distribution arm, Lions Gate Releasing. Formerly Cinepix Film Properties (a thirty-year-old Canadian distribution company Giustra bought in 1997), Lions Gate's Stateside theatrical releasing division is headed by co-presidents Tom Ortenberg and Mark Urman, who have built a reputation for economically distributing and marketing indie fare, including *Gods and Monsters*, *Affliction*, *Buffalo 66*, and *Love and Death on Long Island*. Lions Gate Releasing is a subsid of Lions Gate Films, the Toronto-based production and distribution entity headed by Sackman.

Within a few years of its formation, the fast-growing indie inked output deals with Universal home video and HBO, and formed its own foreign sales arm. In 1998 another LG subsid, Lions Gate Pictures, headed by veteran producers Peter Strauss and John Veitch, took a 45 percent stake in Peter Guber's Mandalay Pictures. But in 1999 Mandalay and LG severed their two-year-old TV production partnership.

PETER SCHNEIDER

President

Walt Disney Studios
500 South Buena Vista St.
Team Disney Building
Burbank, CA 91521
Phone: (818) 560-1000
Fax: (818) 560-8107

In a rare crossover performance, Peter Schneider has moved from animation executive to taking charge of Disney's stage theatricals to now handling live-action films, in addition to the other two. Disney topper Michael Eisner, who adores the exec because he has maintained Disney's animation dominance and made Disney theater into a cash cow for the studio, may have bitten off more than Schneider can chew—as many in the live-action side are betting. Schneider has a steep learning curve in film to overcome, but he is entirely capable, ambitious, and likable (a trait not heaped upon his predecessor at Touchstone and Walt Disney Pictures, David Vogel). Showing that even animation mavens can wage corporate warfare, Schneider won a power struggle with Vogel that left the latter out of a job in April 1999. One of Schneider's first deals as Walt Disney Pictures prexy was to acquire the U.S. rights to David Lynch's G-rated *The Straight Story*—a deal seen as an unlikely pairing between the family banner and one of the industry's most controversial filmmakers.

ROBERT SHAYE

Chairman/CEO

New Line Cinema
888 Seventh Avenue
20th Floor
New York, NY 10106
Phone: (212) 649-4900
Fax: (212) 649-4966

Bob Shaye is cantankerous and blustery in all the wrong ways. However, the executive is business savvy in almost all the right ways. Shaye created New Line in 1967 as an outlet for small, low-budget features like *Reefer Madness*, *Pink Flamingos*, and Jean-Luc Godard's *Sympathy for the Devil*. Since then, New Line Cinema has emerged as a major production player by anyone's standards. The company still depends heavily on its niche genre product to carry it, like *Nightmare on Elm Street*; but ever since Ted Turner bought the company (and then merged with Time Warner in 1996), New Line has mounted a more diverse slate of mainstream offerings, like *The Wedding Singer*, *Austin Powers: The Spy Who Shagged Me*, and the $80 million budgeted *Lost in Space*. Even though he sold off the company to Turner, Shaye still runs the place with a long-term management contract; and furthering his job security, he is said to be tightest with Time Warner vice chairman Turner in the corporate hierarchy.

TOM SHERAK

Chairman of 20th Domestic Film Group/Senior Executive Vice-President Fox Filmed Entertainment

Sherak's flair for showmanship and his relationships with heavyweight filmmakers including George Lucas, Jim Cameron, Chris Columbus, and the *Independence Day* producer/director team of Dean Devlin and Roland Emmerich, earned him the No. 3 exec title at Fox below Peter Chernin and Bill Mechanic. The Brooklyn-born Sherak, who joined Fox in 1983 after a stint as a film buyer for the General Cinema circuit, has a reputation for fierce loyalty and is known

TOM SHERAK (CON'T)

20th Century Fox
10201 West Pico Blvd.
Building 88
Room 109
Los Angeles, CA 90035
Phone: (310) 369-3583
Fax: (310) 369-3155

as one of the true good guys in the business. A sign of the goodwill he has garnered in the community is the millions of dollars he raises annually on behalf of the Multiple Sclerosis Society. His promotion in 1998 to chairman of the newly created Domestic Film Group was perceived by some as a "kick upstairs" to a lofty but empty title. But while Sherak has no day-to-day oversight of any specific division, he remains the point person on some of Fox's biggest releases, most importantly the *Star Wars* franchise.

HOWARD STRINGER

Chairman/CEO

Sony Corporation of America
550 Madison Ave.
34th Floor
New York, NY 10022-3211
Phone: (212) 833-8000
Fax: (212) 833-6777

In December 1998, a jaunty Welshman, Howard Stringer, was upped from president to chairman and CEO, the highest-ranking executive in Sony's U.S. operations. As SCA topper, Stringer is charged with overseeing strategic planning, new business development, and coordination of all Sony's financial and operational activities in the U.S., which include Sony Music Entertainment and Sony Pictures Entertainment. Both SME CEO & chair Thomas D. Mottola and SPE CEO John Calley report to Stringer, rather than to Sony's headquarters in Tokyo—their previous arrangement, which is understood to have hampered negotiations on some business deals. This refined reporting arrangement not only established responsibility for Sony's U.S. operations in a single unit but also gave SCA a single voice in Stringer. The Oxford-educated Vietnam vet arrived on the Sony corporate doorstep in 1997, after serving as chairman and CEO of the telecommunications venture TELE-TV. Stringer preceded TELE-TV with a thirty-year-run with CBS Inc., which he served in a variety of exec roles, including president of the CBS Broadcast Group, where he supervised everything that the network put on the air.

RUTH VITALE AND DAVID DINERSTEIN

Co-Presidents

Paramount Classics
5555 Melrose Avenue
Chevalier Building
Los Angeles, CA 90038
Phone: (323) 956-2000
Fax: (323) 862-1212

It was Paramount topper Jonathan Dolgen who spearheaded the studio's venture into the highly competitive specialized film distribution arena. While he originally wanted to make a deal with Sony Pictures Classics' Michael Barker, Tom Bernard, and Marcie Bloom, whom he had worked with during his Sony days, the trio chose to re-up their deal at Sony instead. So he charged Par vice chairman Rob Friedman with the task of hiring a team of art-house veterans to head the new division. After an extended search, the studio opted in early 1998 for Vitale, then the outgoing president of Fine Line Features, and David Dinerstein, senior VP of marketing at Fox Searchlight. After a relatively slow start (it took nearly a year to announce a name), the company raised its profile on the acquisitions circuit in the spring of 1999. About that time the division released its first film, the narrowly focused British gay coming-of-age pic *Get Real*.

BOB WEINSTEIN

Co-Chairman

Serving for years in the shadow of his older, more gregarious brother, Bob Weinstein is the force behind Dimension, Miramax's lucrative genre label. The co-founder of the distributor of

BOB WEINSTEIN (CON'T)

c/o Miramax/Dimension Films
Tribeca Film Center
375 Greenwich St.
New York, NY 10013
Phone: (212) 941-3800
Fax: (212) 941-3949

such upscale fare as *The English Patient* and *The Piano* admits to liking *The Exorcist* more than *Wings of a Dove*. Dimension got its start in the early '90s with the acquisition of *Halloween V*, but it began to really make noise with the release of Wes Craven's *Scream*, a film credited with the resurgence not only of horror pics but of teen-oriented films in general. Dimension typically accounts for about a third of Miramax's total domestic take, with far fewer films than its artier sister company. While less often in the public spotlight, the younger Weinstein has forged close relationships with filmmakers, including Robert Rodriguez and Quentin Tarantino

HARVEY WEINSTEIN

Co-Chairman

c/o Miramax/Dimension Films
Tribeca Film Center
375 Greenwich St.
New York, NY 10013
Phone: (212) 941-3800
Fax: (212) 941-3949

A master impresario in the mold of P. T. Barnum and Louis B. Mayer, Harvey Weinstein and his brother Bob took art films out of the art houses and turned them into big business. Capitalizing on the major studios' increasing reliance on formula "event pictures" and older, upscale moviegoers' desire for something different, Miramax has turned offbeat fare such as *The Piano*, *The Crying Game*, and *Good Will Hunting* into box office gold. Weinstein's winning combination of good taste and marketing acumen helped the company garner eight Best Picture nominees in eight years, from 1992 to 1999. It also hasn't hurt to have the deep pockets of the corporate parent, the Walt Disney Co., which bought Miramax in 1993 for roughly $60 million. Known as a serious control freak, Weinstein drives his employees to the max—and sometimes beyond.

And while a loyal core of execs has stayed at the company for years, it's conventional wisdom that no one leaves a paying job to go work at Miramax. The former rock concert promoter has reinvented himself of late as a multimedia mogul, socializing with the Pope and Bill and Hillary Clinton and forming *Talk* magazine with uber-editor Tina Brown.

GARETH WIGAN

Co-Vice Chairman

Columbia TriStar Motion Picture Group/Sony Pictures Entertainment

10202 West Washington Blvd.
Thalberg Building
Culver City, CA 90232
Phone: (310) 244-1730
Fax: (310) 244-2626

At sixty-nine, Gareth Wigan is one of the oldest executives in the youth-obsessed film industry. But he is a walking example of the adage that with age comes wisdom. Wigan has been on all sides of the equation in Hollywood: talent agent, producer, and studio executive. He's had huge success as a producer with *The Right Stuff* and *Police Academy*. But those are both so old that industry insiders ask, "What have you done for us lately?" At Sony, Wigan's duties are mainly relegated to international expansion, starting up film divisions in Germany and other countries. He also works with Columbia president Amy Pascal, as do all senior executives, to seek out feature films. Sony chairman John Calley gave him the co-vice-chair title partly because he's one of the few executives who, like Calley, can remember when Coppola was a director and not a wine.

ALEX YEMENIDJIAN

Chairman

CHRIS MCGURK

Vice Chairman

Metro-Goldwyn-Mayer
2500 Broadway
Building F
Santa Monica, CA 90404-3061
Phone: (310) 449-3000

Alex Yemenidjian, a longtime aide to billionaire financier Kirk Kerkorian at both the mogul's private holding company Tracinda and at his hotel concern MGM Grand, was named chairman/CEO of MGM in April 1999, replacing the retiring Frank Mancuso. A day later, Chris McGurk, who had been president of Seagram Co.'s Universal Studios, was named vice chairman/chief operating officer to replace Bob Pisano, who retired along with Mancuso.

Yemenidjian and McGurk were brought in to put some bite back into Leo's sagging jaws, after a prolonged stretch of red ink and box office bombs. Among their first courses of business was to get a decent slate of movies into production, negotiate a possible merger of Metro-Goldwyn-Mayer with a cable programmer, and closely scrutinize the studio's production team and decide if changes needed to be made. The studio is a work in progress, and the verdict is still out whether the duo can overcome MGM's dismal industry perception, which has kept the Lion from attracting top filmmakers and stars to its films.

LAURA ZISKIN

President

A former *D'girl* (Development Girl), Laura Ziskin later distinguished herself as a producer with such pics as *Pretty Woman*, *No Way Out*, and *To Die For*. That distinctive track record led Fox Filmed Entertainment toppers Peter Chernin and Bill Mechanic to tap her in 1994 for the head of Fox 2000, a newly created mainstream production banner aimed at developing and produc-

LAURA ZISKIN (CON'T)

Fox 2000
10201 West Pico Blvd.
Building 78
Los Angeles, CA 90035
Phone: (310) 369-1000
Fax: (310) 369-4258

ing eight to twelve (later cut back to six to eight) wide-appeal films per year. Though she is roundly respected as a producer, as an executive Ziskin has had a bumpy tenure. Among the films Fox 2000 has issued are *Courage Under Fire*, *One Fine Day*, *Inventing the Abbotts*, *Volcano*, *Soul Food*, *The Thin Red Line*, *Ravenous, Pushing Tin*, and *Never Been Kissed*. With only a couple of clear-cut moneymakers among them, Ziskin looked to the release of such films as *The Fight Club*, helmed by David Fincher and starring Brad Pitt and Edward Norton, and *Anna and the King*, starring Jodie Foster and Chow Yun-Fat to turn things around. Despite a long slate of box office disappointments (and despite her rumored desire to want to return to producing), Ziskin continues to have the support of Mechanic, who will most likely allow her to become a producer on the lot, retaining many of the films she has developed as an exec, when her contract expires in 2000. The question then becomes: Does Fox 2000 refer to the label's expiration date or its future freshness?

PRODUCERS

BENDER, Lawrence · BROWN, David · BRUCKHEIMER, Jerry · DAVIS, John · DE LINE, Donald · DEVLIN, Dean · DI NOVI, Denise · GORDON, Lawrence · GRAZER, Brian · HOBERMAN, David · HUGHES, John · HURD, Gale Anne · JERSEY Films (Danny DeVito, Michael Shamberg, and Stacey Sher) · JOHNSON, Mark · JOSEPHSON, Barry · KENNEDY, Kathleen, and Frank Marshall · KOPELSON, Arnold, and Anne Kopelson · LADD, Alan, Jr. · LAWRENCE, Robert · LINSON, Art · MARK, Laurence · NEUFELD, Mace · OBST, Lynda · PETERS, Jon · PRESSMAN, Edward R. · REHME, Robert · ROVEN, Charles · RUDIN, Scott · SHULER-DONNER, Lauren · SILVER, Joel · SIMONDS, Robert · WICK, Douglas · WORKING TITLE Films (Tim Bevan and Eric Fellner) · ZAENTZ, Saul · ZANUCK, Richard · ZWICK, Edward, and Marshall Herskovitz

PRODUCERS

Until the Hollywood studio system came to an end in the early '60s, movie producers were employees of the film companies, just like the directors, writers, and actors they oversaw. Studio toppers with names like Zukor, Mayer, Thalberg, and Zanuck assigned them films, usually with a script, stars, a director, and a budget already in place. The producer's job was simply to see the projects through to completion without spending a nickel more than necessary.

Today's producer is an entirely different, much more entrepreneurial, animal. The studio may provide him an office on the lot and money to pay his phone bills and development staff, but it's the producer's responsibility to seek out material—books, scripts, magazine articles, whatever—and persuade the studio to shell out the hundreds of thousands or even millions of dollars to buy the film rights and pay screenwriters to develop it. With an acceptable script in hand, the producer then has to try to assemble a bankable enough talent package, including a director and stars, to convince the studio to put tens of millions of dollars on the line to greenlight the movie.

Only then does the producer get on with the process of actually putting actors in front of the camera and making a movie.

Top producers are extremely wealthy, but because they spend so much time with hat in hand, very few are perceived as having real power in the industry. A few, though, like Scott Rudin at Paramount, and Brian Grazer at Universal, are such important suppliers of successful product that they wield extraordinary clout at their studios. Their track records also make them a magnet for the best material and top talent. Others, like Mel Gibson's Icon or Cruise-Wagner Prods., get juice from the fact that they are associated with major stars. And then there are producers with a reputation for bringing in projects on time at a reasonable price, which means a lot to studios in an era of shrinking profit margins.

LAWRENCE BENDER

A Band Apart
7966 Beverly Blvd.
Third Floor
Los Angeles, CA 90048
Phone: (323) 951-4600
Fax: (323) 951-4601

In an era when more and more producers find themselves without a studio home, the much-in-demand Bender has two. In addition to a first-look, last-refusal deal with Miramax, for which his and Quentin Tarantino's A Band Apart Prods. has made such profitable pics as *Good Will Hunting* and *Pulp Fiction*, Bender has a second-look deal with Fox 2000. At Fox, where Bender produced *Anna and the King*, starring Jodie Foster and Chow Yun-Fat, he's teamed with former Laurence Mark Prods. exec John Baldecchi. A former dancer who won a scholarship to *Fame* choreographer Louis Falco's dance school, Bender struggled in the late '80s and early '90s as an actor, and in various below-the-line positions before collaborating with Quentin Tarantino on the groundbreaking genre crossover *Reservoir Dogs* (1992). The pair then formed A Band Apart Prods., exec producing Roger Avary's *Killing Zoe* before hitting the big time in 1994 with Tarantino's *Pulp Fiction*, which won the Palme d'Or at the Cannes Film Festival and grossed over $100 million Stateside. Less successful efforts, including *White Man's Burden*, and Boaz Yakin's *Fresh*, followed. He produced, in 1996, *From Dusk Till Dawn*, the Tarantino-scripted, Robert Rodriguez–directed vampire actioner. In 1997, he reteamed with Tarantino for the moderately successful Elmore Leonard adaptation *Jackie Brown*, and also produced the Gus van Sant–helmed hit *Good Will Hunting*, which got nine Academy Award nominations, including one for Best Picture.

DAVID BROWN

Manhattan Project, Ltd.
1775 Broadway
Suite 410
New York, NY 10019-1903
Phone: (212) 258-2541
Fax: (212) 258-2546

Even though he's well into his eighties and based in New York, David Brown is nonetheless a bona fide Hollywood player. In 1998, Brown saw the release of the $350 million worldwide hit *Deep Impact*, which he produced with Steven Spielberg and Richard Zanuck. That same year he went into production with Scott Rudin on *Angela's Ashes*, and with Joe Wizan on *Along Came a Spider* (the sequel to the pair's solid grossing *Kiss the Girls*). The husband of longtime *Cosmo* girl Helen Gurly Brown, Brown was himself at one time managing editor of *Cosmopolitan* before becoming an executive at 20th Century Fox. Through his long partnership with Richard Zanuck, he produced such '70s and '80s hits as *Jaws*, *The Sting*, and *Cocoon*.

JERRY BRUCKHEIMER

Jerry Bruckheimer Films
1631 10th St.
Santa Monica, CA 90404
Phone: (310) 664-6260
Fax: (310) 664-6261

Jerry Bruckheimer and Don Simpson set the trend in Hollywood for the big-budget, high-profile action/adventure film with *Beverly Hills Cop*, *Top Gun*, *Crimson Tide*, *The Rock*, and *Days of Thunder*. Then Simpson went and overdosed, leaving Bruckheimer all by his lonesome. Actually, Bruckheimer was poised to set out on his own anyway, which ultimately led to his producing *Con Air*, *Enemy of the State*, and *Armageddon*. Lately, he's also had *Gone in 60 Seconds* with Nicolas Cage and the independent-minded *Coyote Ugly*. Fact is that Bruckheimer right now is as big as any producer in Hollywood, complete with his own studio space and editing bay in Santa Monica. He also has a humongous deal at Walt Disney

Studios, one of the few full producer arrangements at Disney.

JOHN DAVIS

Davis Entertainment
2121 Avenue of the Stars
Suite 2900
Los Angeles, CA 90067
Phone: (310) 556-3550
Fax: (310) 556-3688

John Davis's entry to Hollywood was opened when his father, oil tycoon Marvin Davis, purchased 20th Century Fox in 1981. Though his father sold the studio in 1985, the Harvard Business School grad had already planted the seeds for a career as a producer, establishing his own production banner, Davis Entertainment, in 1986. Beginning with the 1987 Arnold Schwarzenegger actioner *Predator,* Davis has produced or executive produced more than twenty-five features. While he has never established a clear artistic focus or identifiable imprint on his work, he has achieved great commercial success with such films as *Dr. Dolittle*, *Grumpy Old Men*, its sequel *Grumpier Old Men*, and *The Firm*. Davis's other credits include *Waterworld, Fortress, The Chamber, Daylight,* and the recent Brendan Fraser–starrer, *Dudley Do-Right*. Davis Entertainment currently has a first-look deal with 20th Century Fox, for which Davis has produced *Dr. Dolittle*, *Courage Under Fire*, and *Out to Sea*.

DONALD DE LINE

De Line Pictures
5555 Melrose Ave.
Mae West Building

De Line, a Disney production exec for more than thirteen years, served as president of the studio's Touchstone Pictures label from 1993 until 1998, when he segued into a production deal at Paramount. While at the Mouse House,

DONALD DE LINE (CON'T)

Los Angeles, CA 90038
Phone: (323) 956-3200
Fax: (323) 862-1301

De Line oversaw the development and production of such blockbusters as *Con Air*, *Ransom*, *Sister Act*, and *Pretty Woman*. After his departure from Disney—which coincided with the consolidation of the studio's various production banners—a number of studios vied for his services as a producer, based on his story acumen and relationship with talent. Under his generous three-year, first-look deal at Par, which provides him with a discretionary fund and two senior development execs, he was quick to acquire a number of pricey, high-profile development projects.

DEAN DEVLIN

Centropolis Entertainment
10202 West Washington Blvd.
Astaire Building
Third Floor
Culver City, CA 90232
Phone: (310) 244-4300
Fax: (310) 244-4360

Dean Devlin was often thought of as merely the intern on *L.A. Law*, before turning into the outrageously successful screenwriter and producer of such films as *Stargate*, *Independence Day*, and *Godzilla*. Devlin and director Roland Emmerich met just about 10 years ago on a small film called *Moon 44*, which Emmerich directed. The pair went on to write *Universal Soldier* two years later, followed by three other films, one every two years. Their handiwork led them to a pricey deal at Sony Pictures Entertainment. Only drawback for Devlin is that *Godzilla* didn't really work the way he and Emmerich had planned through their Centropolis Entertainment. So Sony was somewhat irate over the film's overall flop factor. Sony's dissatisfaction with the pic's box office will mean, ultimately, the studio will keep a close eye on Centropolis' next moves.

DENISE DI NOVI

Di Novi Pictures
3110 Main St.
Suite 220
Santa Monica, CA 90405
Phone: (310) 581-1355
Fax: (310) 399-0499

A child who cut her teeth as a TV journalist in Canada, Denise Di Novi made her film debut in 1989, with the dark teen comedy *Heathers*, and then found her true calling with director Tim Burton, running his production company and producing *Edward Scissorhands*, *Batman Returns*, and *The Nightmare Before Christmas*. She shifted to Columbia Pictures on her own to produce *Little Women* and quickly developed a reputation as a tough female producer, who would go to battle with the Joel Silvers of this business when she needed to. Amy Pascal, once president of Turner Pictures, until Turner was folded into Warner Bros., gave Di Novi a three-year deal. Pascal, now president of Columbia, would love to see more of Di Novi at Columbia.

LAWRENCE GORDON

Lawrence Gordon
Productions
c/o Universal Studios
100 Universal City Plaza
Bungalow 424
Universal City, CA 91608
Phone: (818) 777-7933
Fax: (818) 866-5068

Over the years, Mississippi-born Lawrence Gordon has observed Hollywood from myriad positions. He began his career in the early '60s as an assistant to Aaron Spelling before moving on to various exec positions at such companies as ABC Television and Columbia Pictures' feature banner, Screen Gems. Gordon formed his own production company in 1971 and spent more than a decade producing pics such as *The Driver*, *The Warriors*, *Paternity*, and *48 HRS* before taking a job as president and COO of 20th Century Fox in 1984. After leaving the corner office in 1986, Gordon had his most productive run as a producer with such hits as *Field of Dreams*, *Predator*, *Die Hard*, and *Die Hard 2*. In 1989, Gordon founded Largo Entertainment with an influx of cash from Japanese conglomerate JVC Entertainment. His efforts at Largo—whose releases included *Point Break*, *Unlawful Entry*, and *Judgment Night*—paled in comparison with his run as an independent producer, and in 1994, he ankled the now defunct company for a production deal with Universal Pictures. Still going strong, but looking to replicate his pre-Largo success, in recent years Gordon has produced *Devil's Own* and *Event Horizon*, and the 1999 comedy *Mystery Men*, and he's expected to have begun production on the feature version of the hit CD-ROM game *Tomb Raider* by the end of 1999.

BRIAN GRAZER

Imagine Entertainment
1925 Century Park East
Suite 2300
Los Angeles, CA 90067-2734
Phone: (310) 277-1665
Fax: (310) 785-0107

Brian Grazer just might be the strangest chairman in all of Hollywood. Or he's just a fake. The point, with Grazer and his spiked hair, is it's hard to tell what's real and what isn't. The only thing that anyone can truly surmise about him is that he's a hugely successful producer with films like *The Nutty Professor*, *Ransom*, *Apollo 13*, *The Paper*, *Far and Away*, *My Girl*, *Kindergarten Cop*, *Parenthood*, *Splash*, and *Night Shift*. His partnership with director Ron Howard's Imagine Films has helped keep the lights on at Universal Studios, which had a dismal run for most of '98 and '99. With as many as six to eight of its releases in any given year coming from Imagine, Universal has learned to give him what he wants when he wants it. Otherwise, he will take the company to Disney, where Imagine already has a TV deal.

DAVID HOBERMAN

Walt Disney Studios
500 South Buena Vista St.
Burbank, CA 91521-1829
Phone: (818) 560-1000
Fax: (818) 842-4066

A former top production executive at 20th Century Fox, David Hoberman is one of the many dead presidents in town who has been brought back to life in producer form. He caught a wave with *George of the Jungle* and rode it through *I'll Be Home for Christmas*, *Senseless*, *The Negotiator*, and *The Sixth Man*. Now, his deal is shifting toward TV with a pilot called *Monk* and an untitled cop drama for Regency TV and Fox. Though Disney is cutting back on its production deals, his was re-upped by president David Vogel in March 1999. Unfortunately for Hoberman, Vogel was given the axe a month later.

JOHN HUGHES

Hughes Entertainment
1 Westminster Pl.
Lake Forest, IL 60045
Phone: (847) 615-0030
Fax: (847) 615-0587

The director of such '80s teen angst classics as *Ferris Bueller's Day Off*, and *The Breakfast Club*, Hughes has had his biggest hits in the '90s as the writer-producer of broad family comedies like *Home Alone*, *Home Alone 2*, *101 Dalmatians*, and *Flubber*. Still, it's with those earlier pics, on which many of today's young Hollywood execs cut their teeth, that Hughes's name remains synonymous. It's a measure of his clout and prolific output that he was able to ink simultaneous deals with Fox and Warner Bros. in the early '90s. He later followed Fox studio topper Joe Roth to Disney. In the mid-'90s he teamed with ex-Disney exec Ricardo Mestres for nearly three years in the production venture Great Oaks Entertainment. Another sign of Hughes's juice is his ability to make Hollywood come to him: The Chicago-based filmmaker shoots extensively in the Windy City, where he lives and maintains an office.

GALE ANNE HURD

Pacific Western Productions
5555 Melrose Ave.
Lubitsch Annex
Suite 119
Los Angeles, CA 90038
Phone: (323) 956-8601
Fax: (323) 862-1101

A female producer with a taste for macho hardware pics, Hurd had a hand in creating some of the biggest event pics of the '80s and '90s, including sci-fi actioners *Terminator* 1 & 2, *Aliens*, *The Abyss*, and *Armageddon*. She has also served up horror (*Tremors*, *The Relic*) and natural disasters (*Dante's Peak*). But Hurd has also demonstrated a commitment to independent filmmaking, producing the critically acclaimed *The Waterdance*, a drama about a group of men coping with the effects of paralysis, and later serving on the board of the Independent Feature Project/West. Hurd has been married to three industry heavyweights: onetime producing partner and *Titanic* director James Cameron, *Mission: Impossible* helmer Brian De Palma, and *Armageddon* scribe Jonathan Hensleigh. She began her career as an assistant to the legendary B-movie producer-director Roger Corman at New World Pictures before becoming the indie company's head of marketing. Later she produced with Corman the 1981 car chase comedy *Smokey Bites the Dust* before forming her own Pacific Western Prods. the following year.

JERSEY FILMS (DANNY DEVITO, MICHAEL SHAMBERG, AND STACEY SHER)

10351 Santa Monica Blvd.
Suite 200
Los Angeles, CA 90025

Don't ever call it Danny DeVito's Jersey Films. Michael Shamberg won't stand for it. (Stacey Sher doesn't really care what you call it.) But it may as well be, with DeVito attaching himself as an actor, director, or producer to virtually everything Jersey does. Jersey has been up and down in Hollywood with hits like *Pulp Fiction* and *Reality Bites*, and misses like *Feeling Minnesota* and *8 Seconds*. Lately, the company has jumped

JERSEY FILMS (DANNY DEVITO, MICHAEL SHAMBERG, AND STACEY SHER) (CON'T)

Phone: (310) 203-1000
Fax: (310) 203-1010

up the food chain with George Clooney's *Out of Sight* and *Man on the Moon*, starring Jim Carrey as comic Andy Kaufman. As well, Jersey started its own independent label, Jersey Shore, under Jonathan Weisgal. Currently at Universal, the film company may not stay for long. Shamberg was vehement in a letter to Universal brass in 1998 over the poor marketing and distribution of *Out of Sight*. It will all depend on what happens with *Man on the Moon*.

MARK JOHNSON

Mark Johnson Prods.
DreamWorks
100 Universal City Plaza
Building 10
Universal City, CA 91608
Phone: (818) 733-9872
Fax: (818) 733-9870

As producing partner of director Barry Levinson from 1982 to 1994, Johnson's credits include the Oscar-winner *Rain Man* as well as *Good Morning, Vietnam* and *Tin Men*. Since striking out on his own, the soft-spoken filmmaker has notched such prestige pics as *A Little Princess*, *Donnie Brasco*, and the Kevin Costner/Clint Eastwood starrer *A Perfect World*. In 1996, after an unproductive deal at Paramount Pictures expired, Johnson inked a first-look arrangement with DreamWorks. Erudite and mild-mannered, Johnson hardly fits the stereotypes of the *Swimming with Sharks*–style Hollywood producer. Like his former partner, Levinson, Johnson now devotes a portion of his time and attention to the small screen, exec producing the CBS hour-long drama *L.A. Doctors*.

BARRY JOSEPHSON

Barry Josephson hooked up with Barry Sonnenfeld when the first Barry was president of production at Columbia Pictures and the second

BARRY JOSEPHSON (CON'T)

Sonnenfeld/Josephson
500 South Buena Vista St.
Animation Building
Burbank, CA 91521-1854
Phone: (818) 560-0606
Fax: (818) 556-6662

Barry was directing a little film called *Men in Black*. The two hit it off, and soon after *Men in Black* made several hundred million at the box office, the pair suddenly had a lucrative deal at Disney. Though the first two years of the deal have yielded little in film, the company has put *Fantasy Island* and *Maximum Bob* on the air as TV shows. And its first full-length feature, *The Crew*, was recently greenlighted by Disney and George Litto Pictures, with Burt Reynolds and Richard Dreyfuss attached. Josephson had some credit on Sonnenfeld's *Wild Wild West*, but it's not actually a Sonnenfeld/Josephson production. The company is still a year or two away from full fruition. But in the meantime, Josephson is working around the clock to bring money and projects into the company's lavish offices on the Disney lot.

KATHLEEN KENNEDY AND FRANK MARSHALL

c/o The Kennedy/Marshall Company
1351 4th St.
Fourth Floor
Santa Monica, CA 90401
Phone: (310) 656-8400
Fax: (310) 656-8430

The husband-and-wife team of Kathleen Kennedy and Frank Marshall, who co-founded Amblin Entertainment with Steven Spielberg, and produced some of Universal Pictures' biggest blockbusters during the '70s and '80s, returned to the studio to sign a first-look deal in early 1999. Kennedy, a former local San Diego TV chat show producer, got into the film business as assistant to exec producer John Milius on Spielberg's *1941*. Spielberg relied heavily on the duo during the making of such event pics as *Jurassic Park* and the *Indiana Jones* and *Back to the Future* trilogies. Known in the industry for her humor, enthusiasm, and ability to solve problems gracefully, Kennedy is press shy and has flown below the public's radar. The duo has yet to produce a blockbuster in the post-Spielberg era, despite deals at Paramount and Disney, respectively. Their biggest hit was the critically excoriated *Congo*, which Marshall directed.

ARNOLD AND ANNE KOPELSON

Kopelson Entertainment
2121 Avenue of the Stars
Los Angeles, CA 90067
Phone: (310) 369-7500
Fax: (310) 369-7501

Though he was the driving force behind the lucrative '80s teen jiggle franchise *Porky's*, Arnold Kopelson has spent the ensuing years achieving greater cinema legitimacy—which, in Hollywood parlance, translates as becoming "a first-dollar gross player." To that end, in the '80s and early '90s, he enjoyed varying degrees of commercial and critical success with such films as the Academy Award–winner *Platoon*, *Falling Down*, and *The Fugitive*. Kopelson and wife/partner Anne have also produced *Seven*, *Outbreak*, and *Eraser*, all of which contribute to a collective film roster that has earned nearly $2 billion in worldwide box office receipts. Many of these films were made for Warner Bros., where Kopelson had a first-look deal before leaving for Fox in 1997, after signing one of the richest producer deals in studio history. With millions spent on overhead, staffing, and development costs, the five-year exclusive pact also could be one of the biggest busts in history. As of mid-1999, Kopelson has not gotten one film before the cameras at Fox (although four have been released that were developed under his Warner deal, including *The Devil's Advocate* and *A Perfect Murder*), leading insiders to speculate that the deal might not be renewed, at least not at its current level.

ALAN LADD, JR.

c/o The Ladd Co.
Paramount Pictures
5555 Melrose Ave.
Chevalier 117
Los Angeles, CA 90038
Phone: (323) 956-8203
Fax: (323) 862-1115

The former head of 20th Century Fox and MGM, Ladd has been in business exclusively at Paramount since 1993. His credits include the surprise hit *The Brady Bunch Movie* and the Oscar-winning kilt classic *Braveheart*. Ladd's reputation as a dependable producer and his strong relationship with studio chief Sherry Lansing have made him the go-to guy. But he has yet to get onto film an adaptation of Pat Conroy's novel *Beach Music*, which Par bought for him for a reported $1.6 million. While his tenure atop MGM/UA was undistinguished, it was during Ladd's reign at Fox in the mid-'70s that the company released the first two *Star Wars* movies.

ROBERT LAWRENCE

Maysville Pictures
Warner Bros.
4000 Warner Blvd.
Building 81
Burbank, CA 91522
Phone: (818) 954-4840
Fax: (818) 954-4860

Robert Lawrence's stock as a producer skyrocketed after he teamed up with George Clooney. Now, the pair is being very aggressive about new material for Clooney to star in and produce, as well as for Lawrence to produce. High on the agenda are *The Catcher Was a Spy: The Mysterious Life of Moe Berg*, *The Daddy Clock*, *The Castle* (for DreamWorks), and *The Long Walk*. The company is also big within the TV world, with deals at CBS and Warner Bros. TV.

ART LINSON

Linson Films
c/o 20th Century Fox
10201 West Pico Blvd.
Building 86
Los Angeles, CA 90035
Phone: (310) 369-3946
Fax: (310) 369-8515

Over the years, Art Linson has made a name for himself by producing an eclectic slate of films that includes *The Untouchables*, *Fast Times at Ridgemont High*, *Heat*, *Melvin and Howard*, and *Scrooged*. Early in his career, Linson—a former record industry entrepreneur—produced such pics as *Car Wash*, *American Hot Wax*, and *The Wild Life*. Linson, who currently is based at Fox Filmed Entertainment, where he has had a deal since 1995, first under a pact with 20th Century Fox that was later moved to sister banner Fox 2000. For the studio, Linson has produced *Great Expectations*, *The Edge*, *Pushing Tin*, *The Fight Club*, and *Sunset Strip*. While he's regarded as one of those rare full-service producers who can develop, package, and produce films without a lot of hand-holding, those credentials haven't led to many box office hits in recent years. During breaks while producing *This Boy's Life*, Linson wrote his first book, *A Pound of Flesh: Perilous Tales of How to Produce Movies in Hollywood*, an incisive guidebook for aspiring producers.

LAURENCE MARK

Laurence Mark Productions
c/o Columbia Pictures
10202 West Washington Blvd.
Sidney Poitier Building
Culver City, CA 90232
Phone (310) 244-5239
Fax: (310) 244-0061

Laurence Mark began his career as a publicist before segueing into the executive ranks (at Paramount and 20th Century Fox) and later hanging out his own production shingle. Today, Mark has become one of the more prolific producers in Hollywood, with credits that include *Jerry Maguire*, *Anywhere but Here*, and *Romy and Michelle's High School Reunion*. After working as a production exec for several years, Mark founded his production banner at Fox, where he produced *Black Widow* (1987) and exec produced *Working Girl* (1988). In 1989, the company signed a new deal with Walt Disney Studios, where Mark produced such pics as *One Good Cop* (1991), *Cutthroat Island* (1995), *Sister Act 2: Back in the Habit* (1993), and *Simon Birch* (1998). While Mark has had a varied roster of films over the years, he enjoyed his biggest success with the 1996 box office and critical hit *Jerry Maguire*, directed by Cameron Crowe and starring Tom Cruise. Mark also exec produced James L. Brooks's *As Good As It Gets* (1997). In 1998, after eight years as a producer for Disney, Mark moved his company to Columbia Pictures, where he and Nora Ephron are producing the big-screen adaptation of Delia Ephron's book *Hanging Up*, which Diane Keaton directs.

MACE NEUFELD

c/o Mace Neufeld Prods.
Paramount Pictures
5555 Melrose Ave.
Dressing Room Building
Suite 112
Los Angeles, CA 90038
Phone: (323) 956-4816
Fax: (323) 862-2571

During his eight-year partnership with former New World topper Robert Rehme, Neufeld was one half of the producing team behind Paramount's Tom Clancy techno-thrillers *The Hunt for Red October*, *Patriot Games*, and *Clear and Present Danger*. After a brief cold war between Paramount and the bestselling author thawed, Neufeld jumped back on the Jack Ryan bandwagon to develop Clancy's *The Sum of All Fears*. Since the pair parted ways in 1997, Neufeld has produced Par's 1999 release *The General's Daughter* and was anointed to join producer David Brown on *The Saint*, already in progress.

Neufeld's credits in the pre-Rehme days

included *The Omen*, *No Way Out*, *The Frisco Kid*, and *Transylvania 6-5000*.

LYNDA OBST

c/o Paramount Pictures
5555 Melrose Ave.
Los Angeles, CA 90038
Phone: (323) 956-8744
Fax: (323) 862-2287

One-time journalist Obst got her start in 1979 as a development exec for Peter Guber's Casablanca/PolyGram, working on such pics as *Flashdance* and *Clue*. After a stint with the David Geffen Co., Obst partnered with Debra Hill, setting up shop at Paramount, where exec Dawn Steel gave the duo a break. Obst later moved to Columbia, where she produced *The Fisher King* (with Hill) and exec produced *Sleepless in Seattle*. Under a later deal at Fox, her credits included *The Siege*, *Bad Girls*, and *One Fine Day*. The nonfiction book *Hello, He Lied*, Obst's behind-the-scenes look at the film industry, took a magnifying glass to the unspoken power dynamic that informs virtually every word uttered in Hollywood. In 1999, Obst signed an unusual two-tiered deal with Paramount Pictures—for big-budget pics—and Par-based production-financing entity Lakeshore Entertainment—for lower-cost projects.

JON PETERS

Peters Entertainment
4000 Warner Blvd.
Building 15
Burbank, CA 91522
Phone: (818) 954-2441
Fax: (818) 954-4976

Following the brief but terrifying reign of Jon Peters and former producing partner Peter Guber over Sony Pictures Entertainment beginning in 1989 (during which time they overspent and mismanaged their way to a $2.7 billion loss for Sony), many thought (or hoped) that Peters's best days were behind him. With Guber, Peters had produced *Batman* and executive produced

Rain Man in the '80s. After being forced out of Sony by his former partner in 1991, Peters inked a production pact with Columbia and Warner Bros. (where he is now based). On his own, Peters has produced such disappointments as *Money Train*, *My Fellow Americans*, and *Rosewood*. But the former hairdresser hopes to prove that there are indeed second acts in Hollywood with the 1999 summer event pic *Wild Wild West* and another potential franchise, *Superman*, which he's developing with Nick Cage possibly starring. Peters began his film career as personal manager (and boyfriend) of Barbra Streisand; and he quickly made a name for himself with his first outing as a producer, the Streisand hit *A Star Is Born* (1976), which earned four Oscar nominations. The mercurial self-promoter went on to produce *The Main Event* (1979) and *The Eyes of Laura Mars* (1978); and the Guber-Peters duo produced *Vision Quest* (1985), *The Witches of Eastwick* (1987), and *Batman* (1989).

EDWARD R. PRESSMAN

c/o Edward R. Pressman Film Corp.
130 South El Camino Dr.
Beverly Hills, CA 90212
Phone: (310) 271-8383
Fax: (310) 205-6283

With production credits on fifty movies, ranging from the widely praised *Das Boot*, *Badlands*, and *Wall Street* to the commercially successful *The Crow* and *Conan the Barbarian*—not to mention big-budget clunkers *Judge Dredd* and *The Island of Dr. Moreau*—Pressman tends to stay out of the spotlight and is known as a meticulous dealmaker. He puts his money where his mouth is, spending his own cash to develop projects. Pressman is always on the lookout for creative financing techniques (for the vidgame-based actioner

Street Fighter, Pressman got a fat check from Capcom, the game's Japanese manufacturer). In 1997, he partnered with foreign sales outfit Quadra Entertainment, and in 1999 he teamed with *The Thin Red Line* writer-director and recluse Terrence Malick to form Columbine Prods., which inked a three-picture, three-year development and distribution pact with specialized distributor Sony Pictures Classics.

ROBERT REHME

Rehme Productions
11030 Santa Monica Blvd.
Suite 109
Los Angeles, CA 90025
Phone: (310) 477-1991
Fax: (310) 477-3881

Industry vet Rehme has been an exhibitor, a studio exec, a producer, and—on two different occasions—the top-ranking officer of the Academy of Motion Picture Arts & Sciences. During his eight-year partnership with producer Mace Neufeld at Paramount, Rehme produced three successful Tom Clancy techno-thrillers: *The Hunt for Red October*, *Patriot Games*, and *Clear and Present Danger*. But the duo also produced the franchise-killer *Beverly Hills Cop 3*, after which they found it hard to get projects off the ground at Par. The pair parted ways in 1997, and Rehme went on to form feature outfit Rehme Prods. and Phoenix/Rehme Prods., a joint TV venture with Mike Medavoy's Phoenix Pictures. Rehme, who started out in showbiz as a sixteen-year-old theater usher in his native Cincinnati, served as VP of Roger Corman's New World Pictures 1975–78 and as president and chief exec officer of Avco Embassy Pictures 1978–81. He then joined Universal, where he made the shift from president of worldwide distribution and marketing to president of Universal's theatrical motion picture group. From 1983 to 1989 he was co-chairman and CEO of New World Entertainment. A passionate and activist AMPAS president, Rehme supported the push to move the Oscarcast to Sundays, as well as a number of unpopular rules changes by the Oscar-giving org., including the elimination of the Documentary Short category.

CHARLES ROVEN

Atlas Entertainment
227 Broadway
Suite 300
Santa Monica, CA 90401
Phone: (310) 724-7719
Fax: (310) 576-0799

Chuck Roven was married to former Columbia Pictures and Paramount Pictures heavyweight Dawn Steel, who died of a brain tumor in 1998. The company the two of them built, meanwhile, put out *City of Angels* and *Fallen* at Warner Bros. in 1998. Three years earlier, the company was handling *Angus* and *Twelve Monkeys*. Roven has always been a force in features and TV. With a slew of projects in development, it looks as though Roven and Atlas will maintain their spot at Warner Bros. A few titles include *The Grabbers*, *The Defective Detective*, *Safe Conduct*, *Foundation*, *The Zen Differential*, *The Pledge*, and *The Killer*.

SCOTT RUDIN

Scott Rudin Prods.

One of the most respected producers in Hollywood and New York—he has offices on both coasts—Rudin is known for his bulldog tenacity and superb taste in material. He's also known for his stormy and at times vindictive temper, and a take-no-prisoners approach that strikes fear in the hearts of otherwise confident industryites.

SCOTT RUDIN (CON'T)

120 West 45th St.
Tenth Floor
New York, NY 10036
Phone: (212) 704-4600
Fax: (212) 869-8557

But even his critics admit that battles with Rudin are mostly about improving the quality of the film, not the usual ego-stroking skirmishes over perks or credits. And no one can deny the success of Rudin's eclectic oeuvre, which includes such unlikely hits as *The First Wives Club*, *In & Out*, and *The Truman Show*. In a town where many producers grow old waiting for a green light, Rudin had six pictures in various stages of production in 1999. While he's notorious for making his assistants' lives miserable—he supposedly let one out on the freeway after the underling had failed to let the car interior cool down adequately—working for Rudin has become as much of a rite of passage in Hollywood as the William Morris mailroom, and the names of his ex-associates make up a junior power list.

LAUREN SHULER-DONNER

Donner/Shuler-Donner Productions
4000 Warner Blvd.
Building 103
Room 4
Burbank, CA 91522
Phone: (818) 954-3961
Fax: (818) 954-4908

Shuler-Donner had paid her dues and even produced a hit movie—the 1983 John Hughes–penned, Michael Keaton–starrer *Mr. Mom*—before teaming up with future partner and husband Richard Donner on the 1985 actioner *Ladyhawke*. Later feature credits include Joel Schumacher's *St. Elmo's Fire* (1985), the Howard Deutch–helmed *Pretty in Pink* (1986), and Donner's *Radio Flyer* (1992), as well as such box-office hits as *Dave*, *Free Willy 1 & 2*, and 1998's *You've Got Mail*. After getting her start editing medical films and working as a camera operator on rock concerts and sitcoms, Shuler segued in the mid-'70s into production on

ABC's *Wide World of Entertainment*. She then became a story editor at Motown Films, where she later made her TV producing debut on the 1979 Schumacher-helmed telepic *Amateur Night at the Dixie Bar and Grill*.

JOEL SILVER

Silver Pictures
c/o Warner Bros.
4000 Warner Blvd.
Building 90
Burbank, CA 91522
Phone: (818) 954-4490
Fax: (818) 954-3237

Silver is best known as the unapologetic producer of formulaic, violent, if often entertaining action films of the late '80s and early '90s, most notably the lucrative *Lethal Weapon* franchise. After a career lull in the mid-'90s, Silver's cachet was revived in 1999 after he shepherded the cutting-edge cyber-actioner *The Matrix*. Silver broke into the business in the late '70s as an assistant to producer Larry Gordon, and was later promoted to president of Gordon's feature company. While there, he got an associate producer credit on 1979's *The Warriors* and produced the 1982 buddy cop pic *48 HRS*. In 1985, he unfurled his own Silver Pictures banner, producing the macho-actioner *Commando*. But it was with Richard Donner's 1987 Mel Gibson–Danny Glover action-comedy *Lethal Weapon* that Silver blasted his way to the top of the Hollywood heap. The pic was followed by three sequels over the next twelve years, each of which grossed over $100 million domestically. But later big-budget efforts, including Donner's *Assassins* (scripted by *The Matrix*–helmers Larry and Andy Warchowski) and the Gibson-starrer *Conspiracy Theory*, offered less spectacular returns. Silver was an exec producer, along with Donner, David Giler, Walter Hill, and Robert Zemeckis, of the long-running HBO series *Tales from the Crypt*, for which he directed an episode in 1992. Silver re-teamed with Zemeckis in 1999 on the Warners Bros.–based mid-budget horror feature venture Dark Castle Entertainment, whose first project was a remake of the classic chiller *House on Haunted Hill*. Dark Castle retains international rights to its pics, with London-based J&M Entertainment handling foreign sales. A potentially lucrative deal for the filmmakers—although overseas audiences are notoriously indifferent to horror pics.

ROBERT SIMONDS

The Robert Simonds Co.
100 Universal City Plaza
Building 507A
Penthouse 1
Universal City, CA 91608-1085
Phone: (818) 777-5445
Fax: (818) 866-1404

Bob Simonds produced four films in 1998, two of them absolute blockbusters—*The Wedding Singer* and *The Waterboy*. Two others were utter disasters—*Half-Baked* and *Dirty Work*. Only the disastrous *Half-Baked* was released by Universal, which was so desperate for a Simonds hit, the studio was willing to give him any production requirement he requested. His current deal at Universal has near greenlight capability, though he still has yet to come up with anything major. Though *OO-Soul* looked like it was on track to be made with Chris Tucker, the whole project fell apart over egos. Though Simonds was rumored for a short time to be taking Casey Silver's former spot as head of Universal Pictures, those closer to the top figured that rumor to be homespun, coming from Simonds himself. He currently has fifteen to twenty projects in development that he's targeting for studio life.

DOUGLAS WICK

Red Wagon Films
10202 West Washington Blvd.
Capra #112
Culver City, CA 90232
Phone: (310) 244-4466
Fax: (310) 244-1480

Doug Wick is not only producing a number of high-profile Columbia Pictures films; he's also married to the vice-chair of the studio, Lucy Fisher. Wick made a name for himself on *Working Girl*, starring Harrison Ford, and on *Wolf*, starring Jack Nicholson. He has a slew of projects in production, pre-production, or development. They include an untitled Ford project, *The Hollow Man*, *Stuart Little*, *Memoirs of a Geisha* with Steven Spielberg, *Gladiator*, *Girl Interrupted* from director James Mangold with Winona Ryder, *Fever*, *Bewitched*, and *A Simple Wedding*. Wick is a legitimate force for Sony, which is why his deal is there to stay when so many others are being tossed out like yesterday's garbage.

WORKING TITLE FILMS

Tim Bevan and Eric Fellner
Co-Chairmen
9333 Wilshire Blvd.
Beverly Hills, CA 90210
Phone: (310) 777-3100
Fax: (310) 777-4698

Working Title, which produced such hugely profitable features as *Four Weddings and a Funeral*, *Fargo*, *Dead Man Walking*, and *Notting Hill*, remains one of the few (the only?) non-U.S.-based companies with a consistent track record of international hits. As WT co-chairmen Tim Bevan and Eric Fellner's deal with PolyGram was about to expire, Hollywood studios scrambled to secure their services. The duo eventually signed a five-year pact with Universal (which bought PolyGram in 1999) giving them greenlight power over pics with budgets of up to $25 million. But because the fiercely independent filmmakers were bent on maintaining their distance from Hollywood, the company's production, development, and operational costs are co-financed on a 50–50 basis with French powerhouse Canal Plus, with distribution rights allocated through a complex formula. In May 1999, Working Title launched a low-budget development and production division, dubbed WT2, focusing on projects budgeted under $5 million and headed by production execs John Finn and Natascha Wharton.

SAUL ZAENTZ

The Saul Zaentz Co.
2600 10th St.
Berkeley, CA 94710
Phone: (510) 549-2500
Fax: (510) 486-2015

A literal Hollywood outsider, Zaentz is based in the San Francisco Bay area along with such filmmaking iconoclasts as George Lucas and Francis Ford Coppola. Zaentz, who divides his time between the music and film industries, is not a prodigious producer—he has made just ten films in a quarter-century. But he puts his money where his mouth is, financing development himself and thus avoiding the de-flavorizing effect of endless studio story meetings. Also, unlike insiders whose careers hinge on playing politics, Zaentz frequently criticizes the majors for their typically safe, low-brow approach to material. He also publicly excoriated Fox execs for pulling out of *The English Patient* days before production was to begin. His risk-taking has resulted in three Oscar Best Picture winners: *The English Patient*, *Amadeus*, and *One Flew over the Cuckoo's Nest*. Zaentz is credited as exec producer on New Line's ambitious live-action adaptation of J. R. R. Tolkien's *Lord of the Rings* trilogy, the rights to which Zaentz optioned for an animated version he produced in 1978. Zaentz's temperament has put him at odds with creative types at times, most famously in the long-running legal disputes with singer-songwriter John Fogerty, who recorded for Zaentz's Fantasy Records in the early '70s.

RICHARD ZANUCK

The Zanuck Company
9465 Wilshire Blvd.
Suite 930
Beverly Hills, CA 90212
Phone: (310) 274-0261
Fax: (310) 273-9217

Richard Zanuck has the distinction of being the 20th Century Fox production topper who was handed his walking papers in 1970 by his own father, studio legend Darryl F. Zanuck. Not long after being fired by Pop, Zanuck bounced back by producing a series of hits, including the 1975 blockbuster *Jaws* and *Jaws 2* with partner David Brown, who also produced the $350 million grosser *Deep Impact* for Paramount/Dream-Works. At sixty-five, Zanuck is still one of the town's more prolific producers, with such recent credits as the Clint Eastwood thriller *True Crime* and the William Friedkin–helmed *Rules of Engagement*, which he produced with Scott Rudin. One of Zanuck's most lauded pictures, *Driving Miss Daisy*, which won Best Picture in 1989, was the debut feature of the Zanuck Co., which Zanuck formed with his wife after he and Brown ended their partnership in 1988. Having dealt with filmmaking as an exec and as an indie producer, Zanuck's been able to see the strengths and lunacies of both the old system and the current one. "What kills the business today is that everybody overdevelops everything," Zanuck told *Variety* in 1998. "In my day, we always made everything that we bought."

EDWARD ZWICK AND MARSHALL HERSKOVITZ

Bedford Falls Company
409 Santa Monica Blvd.
Santa Monica, CA 90401
Phone: (310) 394-5022
Fax: (310) 394-5825

Writer-director-producers Edward Zwick and Marshall Herskovitz first teamed on the 1983 NBC telepic *Special Bulletin*, which Zwick directed and co-wrote and co-produced with Herskovitz. Two years later they formed the Bedford Falls Company, under which Zwick and Herskovitz have produced such TV fare as *thirtysomething*, *My So-Called Life*, and *Relativity*, and such features as *Legends of the Fall*, *Dangerous Beauty,* and *The Siege*. Bedford Falls currently has a first-look production deal with Fox Filmed Entertainment's Fox 2000 division. Zwick, who directed the Civil War saga *Glory* in 1989, also directed *About Last Night . . .*, *Leaving Normal*, *Legends of the Fall*, *Courage Under Fire*, and *The Siege*. Zwick, a former editor and feature writer for *The New Republic* and *Rolling Stone* magazines, also served as a producer on the Oscar-winner *Shakespeare in Love*. Herskovitz, who began his career as a writer on the TV series *Family*, *The White Shadow*, and *Seven Brides for Seven Brothers*, segued into feature directing with *Jack the Bear* in 1993. He also directed the period romance *Dangerous Beauty* in 1998.

HYBRIDS

(Producers/Financiers)

BARBER, Gary, and Roger Birnbaum (Spyglass Entertainment) · BERMAN, Bruce (Village Roadshow Pictures) · BERNSTEIN, Armyan (Beacon Communications) · GORDON, Mark, and Gary Levinsohn (Mutual Film Company) · GUBER, Peter, and Adam Platnick (Mandalay Pictures) · HOPE, Ted, David Linde, and James Schamus (Good Machine) · MEDAVOY, Mike (Phoenix Pictures) · MILCHAN, Arnon (New Regency Productions · REUTHER, Steve (Bel Air Entertainment) · ROBINSON, James (Morgan Creek Productions) · ROSENBERG, Tom (Lakeshore Entertainment Corp.) · SAMAHA, Elie (Franchise Pictures) · STABLER, Steve (Destination Films) · WOODS, Cary (Independent Pictures)

HYBRIDS

(Producers/Financiers)

As multiplexes and satellite dishes proliferate on virtually every rue and strasse around the globe, the worldwide appetite for A-level American feature films continues to increase. Because the U.S. majors all typically distribute their own films internationally, local independent distributors are particularly hungry for star-driven product. As the cost of making and marketing movies spiraled out of control in the late '90s, studios anxious to limit their financial exposure on any one picture began looking for co-financing partners to shoulder some of the risk.

Responding to these two simultaneous conditions, a number of globally savvy producers and moneymen formed feature production companies backed by foreign investment and a domestic studio distribution deal.

For lack of a better word, we have categorized these ventures—and the entrepreneurs who run them—as hybrids: a cross between a studio-based production company, a foreign sales outfit, and a self-contained studio. Typically these entities partner with a handful of overseas distributors and/or satellite TV companies, who pony up francs, yen, marks or lire, in exchange for the right to distribute the films in their own territories—plus a stake in worldwide profits. Additional capital may come from bank financing, equity investors, or more esoteric financial arrangements, such as insurance policies and tax rebates.

In the U.S., hybrids often ink a "service" deal with a studio, whereby the company pays a fee to rent the studio's distribution system, as well as handling its own marketing costs.

For better or worse, one of the forerunners of this approach was probably Carolco, the high-flying indie of the '80s that funded such blockbusters as *Terminator 2: Judgment Day* and *Rambo* by preselling the rights to indie distributors overseas. Eventually, Mario Kassar and Andy Vajna's free-spending company—which owned a jet and a lavish yacht, and outspent the studios to get top star talent—collapsed under the weight of such as costly disasters as *Chaplin* and *Cutthroat Island*.

Today's hybrids are considerably more prudent affairs that count on long-term partnerships with foreign distributors rather than presales—and less princely perks. But there are still no guarantees of success.

Nevertheless, agents and creative types welcome the birth of these players because it increases the number of buyers at a time when studios are tightening their belts.

GARY BARBER AND ROGER BIRNBAUM

Spyglass Entertainment
500 South Buena Vista St.
Burbank, CA 91521
Phone: (818) 560-3458
Fax: (818) 563-4625

Gary Barber and Roger Birnbaum came together in 1998 to create Spyglass Entertainment. The company is quickly turning into a major label of its own with foreign financing and output deals with numerous territories. Barber, an Aussie who had previously been with Morgan Creek Prods., and Birnbaum, who at one point ran Caravan with Joe Roth, united to create this Disney-based entity. The company is one of several in town that find outside money through foreign deals to fully finance high-profile, big-ticket films. And the pedigree is decent enough—Birnbaum's producing credits include *While You Were Sleeping*, *Powder*, *Angels in the Outfield*, and *Grosse Point Blank;* Barber's executive produced credits include *Major League*, *Ace Ventura: Pet Detective*, *Two If by Sea*, and *Ace Ventura: When Nature Calls*.

BRUCE BERMAN

Chairman/CEO

Berman, who rose through the ranks from VP to president of worldwide production during his twelve-year career at Warner Bros., became the

BRUCE BERMAN (CON'T)
Village Roadshow Pictures
c/o Warner Bros.
4000 Warner Blvd.
Burbank, CA 91522
Phone: (818) 954-1998
Fax: (818) 954-1959

chairman and CEO of L.A.-based Village Roadshow Pictures in late 1997. He joined the subsidiary of twenty-five-year-old Australian studio Village Roadshow at the same time it inked a five-year, twenty-picture co-financing venture with WB. The pact called for Roadshow to commit $250 million for production and about half as much again for prints and advertising. Warners handles worldwide distribution rights to the pictures in all territories except Village Roadshow's home turf of Australia and New Zealand. The partnership got off to a rip-roaring start with the 1999 hits *The Matrix* and *Analyze This*, as well as the moderately successful 1998 chick pic *Practical Magic*. Berman started out in assistant roles to MPAA chairman Jack Valenti, Casablanca founder Peter Guber, and producers Sean Daniel and Joel Silver at Universal, where he later became production VP. He joined WB as a veep in 1984 and was upped to president in 1989, shepherding such blockbusters as *The Fugitive* and *Twister* before segueing in 1996 into a short-lived production deal with the studio. Many of the Village Roadshow pics are culled from WB projects put into development under Berman's watch. As Berman himself once put it: "I don't think there's anyone that knows the inventory better than I do."

ARMYAN BERNSTEIN

Beacon Communications

Army Bernstein has quietly watched his Beacon Pictures go from small indie feature house (*The Commitments*) to a mini-major with *Air Force One* having earned more than $300 million

ARMYAN BERNSTEIN (CON'T)

Warner-Hollywood Studios
1040 North Formosa Ave.
Hollywood, CA 90046-6798
Phone: (323) 850-2651
Fax: (323) 850-2613

worldwide. Now, the company makes its choice of feature mega-films with name stars, such as *End of Days* with Arnold Schwarzenegger and *Thirteen Days* with Kevin Costner. Bernstein has also led a buyback of the company from Ascent Entertainment and plans to move into TV and talent management. Beacon suffered a a small setback in 1998 with the defection of production chief Jon Shestack to Artisan Entertainment. But Bernstein and his second, Marc Abraham, are confident that they can set up more A-list, studio projects with all their foreign dough.

MARK GORDON AND GARY LEVINSOHN

Mutual Film Company
Raleigh Studios
650 North Bronson Ave.
Clinton Building
Hollywood, CA 90004
Phone: (323) 871-5690
Fax: (323) 871-5689

Speed producer Gordon and foreign finance guru Levinsohn (*Twelve Monkeys*) teamed up in late 1995 to form the Paramount-based Mutual Film Co. (originally called Cloud Nine). Investing funds on behalf of its overseas distribution and equity partners—U.K.'s BBC, Japan's Toho-Towa and Marubeni, Germany's TeleMunchen, and France's UGC—the company has partially bankrolled such pics as *A Simple Plan*, *Patriot*, and *Primary Colors*. The Mutual team also produces films it doesn't co-finance, including DreamWorks' modest kid pic *Paulie: A Parrot's Tale*. The company has its own foreign sales arm to handle territories not covered by its distribution partners.

PETER GUBER AND ADAM PLATNICK

Guber, the ex-Sony Pictures chairman who oversaw the studio's disastrous $3.2 billion loss,

PETER GUBER AND ADAM PLATNICK (CON'T)
Mandalay Pictures
c/o Paramount Pictures
5555 Melrose Ave.
Jerry Lewis Building
Los Angeles, CA 90038
Phone: (323) 956-2400
Fax: (323) 862-2266

formed Mandalay Entertainment with a hefty investment from his Japanese former bosses. He teamed with international finance veteran Adam Platnick to form a new kind of company that finances its own films and then licenses distribution rights to a studio domestically and to foreign distributors through its partnerships overseas. At Sony the company was responsible for such successes as *Donnie Brasco*, *Seven Years in Tibet*, and *I Know What You Did Last Summer*. In 1997, Mandalay moved to Par (and changed its name to Mandalay Pictures), where it produced Tim Burton's *Sleepy Hollow*.

TED HOPE, DAVID LINDE, AND JAMES SCHAMUS

Good Machine
417 Canal Street
Fourth Floor
New York, NY 10013
Phone: (212) 343-9230
Fax: (212) 343-9645

Touted as the only U.S. production company with a foreign sales arm, Gotham-based Good Machine was founded in 1991 by Ted Hope and James Schamus, who met while working as script readers for New Line Cinema. Since then the duo has produced such critically lauded films as Ang Lee's *Ice Storm*, *The Wedding Banquet*, *Pushing Hands*, and *Eat Drink Man Woman*. The filmmaker-friendly partners also exec produced Todd Haynes's *Safe*, Cindy Sherman's *Office Killer*, Bart Freundlich's *The Myth of Fingerprints*, John O'Hagan's *Wonderland*, and Edward Burns's debut, *The Brothers McMullen*. In 1996, Hope and Schamus brought on former Miramax exec David Linde to launch Good Machine International, the company's foreign sales arm. While the production arm has a first-look deal with Universal Pictures (for which GM produced Lee's *Ride with the Devil*), with the sale of October Films (a former exclusive supplier to GMI) to Barry Diller's USA Films in 1999, Good Machine International has no obligations to any U.S. distributors, enabling the label to cherry-pick the projects it wants to handle and freely acquire films for domestic sales. GMI also generates revenue with which the production side can finance independent films, making the company a threat on both the festival circuit and in the multiplexes. In addition to his producer duties, Schamus's screenwriting credits include a collaboration with Ang Lee on the Oscar-nominated foreign film *The Wedding Banquet* (1993); and individually, the adaptations of Rick Moody's novel *The Ice Storm* and Daniel Woodrell's novel *Woe to Live On* (released as *Ride with the Devil*), both helmed by Lee.

MIKE MEDAVOY

Chairman/CEO
Phoenix Pictures
10202 West Washington Blvd.
Frankovich Building
Third Floor
Culver City, CA 90232
Phone: (310) 839-8915
Fax: (310) 244-6106

Given his background as a former superagent, Orion Pictures co-founder, and TriStar Pictures chairman, Medavoy had a surprisingly rough time of it during the first few years heading up Phoenix Pictures, his own Sony-based hybrid. The company, founded in 1995, was one of the first to employ an insurance policy to protect its financial downside. But Phoenix achieved little box office traction with its initial releases, including Milos Forman's *The People vs. Larry Flynt* (1996), Barbra Streisand's *The Mirror Has Two Faces* (1996), Oliver Stone's *U-Turn* (1997), Bryan Singer's *Apt Pupil,* and Terrence Malick's *The Thin Red Line*. Born to Russian parents in China in 1941, Medavoy settled in the

U.S. as a teenager and started his showbiz career in the Universal Studios mailroom at age 22. He was soon on his way to top agenting posts at General Artists Corp. and Creative Management Agency, with a client list that boasted Jane Fonda, Michelangelo Antonioni, Francis Ford Coppola, and Steven Spielberg. In 1974, Medavoy made the switch from seller to buyer, joining United Artists as senior VP, and overseeing such Best Picture Oscar-winners as *One Flew over the Cuckoo's Nest*, *Rocky*, and *Annie Hall*. In 1978, Medavoy and four of his UA colleagues defected to found Orion Pictures—in concert with Warner Communications—eventually churning out such Oscar-winners as *Amadeus* (1984) and *Platoon* (1986), and the box-office hit *Robocop* (1987). In 1990, Medavoy took over as chairman of TriStar Pictures. During his somewhat inconsistent four-year watch, TriStar released Carolco's blockbuster sequel *Terminator 2: Judgment Day*, *Hook*, *Basic Instinct*, *Philadelphia*, and *Sleepless in Seattle*.

ARNON MILCHAN

New Regency Productions
10201 West Pico Blvd.
Building 12
Los Angeles, CA 90035
Phone: (310) 369-8300
Fax: (310) 969-0470

Milchan, a British- and Swiss-educated Israeli who fought in the Israeli army before taking over his father's fertilizer company, heads up New Regency Prods., which serves as a prototype for many newer hybrids. The company is partially owned by Rupert Murdoch's NewsCorp., Australia's Kerry Packer, South Korea's Samsung, and German media giant Kirch Group. The company, which began a fifteen-year deal with Fox in

1998, finances two-thirds of its pics itself, and co-finances the balance with Fox, which distributes the pics worldwide, excluding those foreign territories represented by New Regency's investors (or partners). With its massive $600 million credit line with Chase Securities and Berliner Bank, Regency also pays the costs of releasing its films.

Milchan started his showbiz career in Paris, producing plays and TV commercials. His first decade of feature producing yielded such critically lauded work as Martin Scorsese's *King of Comedy*, Terry Gilliam's *Brazil*, and *The War of the Roses*). Later highlights include *Pretty Woman* (1990), *JFK* (1991), *Under Siege* (1992), *Free Willy* (1993), *The Client* (1994), *Heat* (1995), *A Time to Kill* (1996), and *L.A. Confidential* (1997).

In March 1999, Milchan's Regency joined forces with the U.K.'s FilmFour Ltd. and Gallic web TF1 to form an unnamed worldwide production and distribution partnership pledging to bankroll three low-to-medium-budget, English-language European-produced pics per year. Though Milchan is helping Fox enlarge its distribution pipeline while limiting its risk, the savvy entrepreneur isn't putting all his eggs in one basket. In addition to music and TV holdings, Milchan owns a significant minority stake in German actionwear brand Puma AG.

STEVE REUTHER

Bel Air Entertainment

Warner Bros.

Following in the footsteps of his former employer, New Regency topper Arnon Milchan, Reuther has his Warner Bros.–based production

STEVE REUTHER (CON'T)

4000 Warner Blvd.
Burbank, CA 91522
Phone: (818) 954-4040
Fax: (818) 954-2838

and co-financing company Bel-Air Entertainment combine cash investments from foreign distributors with a major U.S. studio output deal. Formed in 1998, Bel Air is backed in part by French pay TV powerhouse Canal Plus, Spanish media conglom Sogecable, and Warners. Early on, the company used its deep pockets to buy a lot of high-profile material, but got off to an undistinguished start with its first co-production, the 1999 Kevin Costner–starrer *Message in a Bottle*. Bel Air is the second hybrid venture headed by Reuther, who in the mid-90s partnered with actor-producer Michael Douglas and German financier Bodo Scriba in Paramount-based Constellation Films. But after producing Par's Francis Ford Coppola–helmed *The Rainmaker* and the Val Kilmer–Michael Douglas starrer *The Ghost and the Darkness*, that venture came to an abrupt end when the German funds suddenly evaporated.

JAMES ROBINSON

Morgan Creek Productions
4000 Warner Blvd.
Building 76
Burbank, CA 91522
Phone: (818) 954-4800
Fax: (818) 954-4811

James Robinson was running Morgan Creek with Gary Barber until mid-1997, when Barber departed to start up Spyglass with Roger Birnbaum. For Morgan Creek and Robinson, this was a significant loss, because Barber was the main reason that Morgan Creek had all the foreign financing deals. Still, Robinson seems to be moving things along with various projects, not the least of which is John Travolta's *Battlefield Earth*, based on L. Ron Hubbard's sci-fi novel. After a slow-moving year with *Soldier* and *Major League: Back to the Minors*, Morgan Creek could certainly use a blockbuster.

TOM ROSENBERG

Lakeshore Entertainment Corp.
Paramount Pictures
5555 Melrose Ave.
Gloria Swanson Building
Los Angeles, CA 90038
Phone: (323) 956-4222
Fax: (323) 862-1190

Chicago insurance and real estate magnate Rosenberg and fellow Windy City businessman Ted Tannebaum formed Paramount-based Lakeshore Entertainment in 1995. The company has a first-look domestic distribution deal with Paramount for films priced over $10 million, but it can go elsewhere with its smaller pics—and any that Paramount turns down. Under the presidency of Propaganda co-founder Joni Sighvatsson, from 1995 to 1998, Lakeshore leaned toward smaller, director-driven—and frankly, less commercial—fare such as Tom DiCello's *Box of Moonlight* and Alain Berliner's *Passion of Mind*. But it was the more mainstream Rosenberg who negotiated a pricey deal to reunite the *Pretty Woman* duo of Julia Roberts and Richard Gere to star in Lakeshore and Par's *Runaway Bride*. Lakeshore retains foreign rights to its films and has its own international sales division. No newcomer to the industry, Rosenberg previously founded the motion picture financing and production company Beacon Communications, which he sold in 1994. Rosenberg, who generally avoids the media spotlight, has clashed with a number of key employees, resulting in defections.

ELIE SAMAHA

Chairman
Franchise Pictures
8228 Sunset Blvd.
Suite 307
Los Angeles, CA 90046
Phone: (323) 822-0730
Fax: (323) 822-2165

Samaha, a Sunset Strip real estate magnate and former owner of the celeb-friendly Roxbury nightclub, has in a few short years become one of Hollywood's most prolific—if not its most successful—producers. In partnership with actor and B-movie producer Andrew Stevens (and earlier with producer Ashok Armitraj), Samaha formed sales and production entity Franchise Pictures. The company, which has a domestic output deal with Morgan Creek and Warner Bros., has quickly distinguished itself from the pack of schlocky foreign sales outfits by bankrolling a number of big-budget, star-driven projects. These include the $80 million sci-fi action-adventure *Battlefield Earth*, starring John Travolta, and the Bruce Willis–Matthew Perry starrer *The Whole Nine Yards*, as well as smaller, prestige projects such as *Hospitality Suite*, starring Kevin Spacey and Danny DeVito, and Agnieszka Holland's *The Third Miracle*, starring Ed Harris and Armin Mueller-Stahl. Early on, Samaha bankrolled Myles Berkowitz's ultra-low-budget mockumentary *20 Dates*, which features a running, audio-only, battle between the filmmaker and the increasingly impatient producer, who pushes Berkowitz to use real actresses like Tia Carrere (Samaha's wife) to increase the pic's foreign sales potential. In collaboration with foreign sales and production outfit Nu Image, he produced Peter Markel's *The Last Days of Frankie the Fly*, starring Dennis Hopper and Daryl Hannah. Samaha was also at one time a partner in Millennium Films, at the time a co-venture with NuImage and October Films.

STEVE STABLER

Destination Films
1299 Ocean Ave.
Fifth Floor
Santa Monica, CA 90401
Phone: (310) 434-2700
Fax: (310) 434-2701

As co-founder with Brad Krevoy of indie production and financing outfit Motion Picture Corp. of America, Stabler produced dozens of pics in the 1990s, including successful broad comedies *Dumb and Dumber*, *Beverly Hills Ninja*, and *Kingpin*. (*Dumb* co-directors Peter and Bobby Farrelly paid homage to the erstwhile partners in *There's Something About Mary* by dubbing two menacing police officers Krevoy and Stabler.) But after MPCA was bought by Orion Pictures—which in turn was swallowed by MGM—the pair went through a distinctly unamicable divorce. Stabler partnered in 1998 with former DreamWorks exec Brent Baum to form domestic distribution and production company Destination Films, partial funding for which was secured through an unusual insurance-backed bond offering. The company acquires and co-produces low-to-moderately priced films, usually splitting worldwide rights with international sales-backed partners. Early projects included a feature version of British kid franchise *Thomas the Tank Engine*. While industryites are split on the soundness of the venture's strategy, the amiable Stabler is generally well-liked. And besides, a new buyer with cash is always welcome in Hollywood.

CARY WOODS

Chairman

Independent Pictures

6161 Santa Monica Blvd.

Suite 100

Los Angeles, CA 90038

Phone: (323) 860-9190

Fax: (323) 860-9180

Woods, whose work as a producer under a deal with Miramax yielded *Swingers*, *Cop Land*, and *Scream*, set up his Independent Pictures in 1997. With equity investments of roughly $40 million—including a $10 million cash infusion from New Line Cinema—and a $50 million line of credit from Chase Manhattan Bank, Woods has set out to build a library by fully financing films without preselling foreign rights. Domestically, Independent inked a five-year deal with New Line in 1998 to distribute four pics per year in most media on a rent-a-system basis. Like a small-scale New Regency, Independent handles the costs and creative elements of marketing. Woods's taste ranges from the radically uncommercial (*Gummo*) to event pics (in 1993, Woods and his then-partner Rob Fried helped convince Japanese major Toho to license the remake rights to *Godzilla* to Sony). But Independent will confine its acquisitions and productions to features in the $1 million to $15 million range. First productions include Mark Hanslon's *Buddy Boy* and Harmony Korine's *The Julien Chronicles*. Independent Pictures acquired U.S. rights to Bruce McCulloch's *Dog Park*, starring Natasha Henstridge, Janeane Garofalo, and Luke Wilson. Woods, who was born in 1958, began his career as an agent at William Morris, where he worked with such clients as Tim Robbins, Uma Thurman, Timothy Hutton, Sandra Bernhard, and Gus Van Sant. Later he joined Sony as vice-president in the office of vice-chairmen Peter Guber and Jon Peters before forming Fried-Woods Prods.

HELMERS
(Directors)

ALLEN, Woody · BAY, Michael · BEATTY, Warren · BESSON, Luc · BROOKS, James L. · BURTON, Tim · CAMERON, James · COEN, Joel, and Ethan Coen · COLUMBUS, Chris · COPPOLA, Francis Ford · CRAVEN, Wes · CROWE, Cameron · DARABONT, Frank · DE BONT, Jan · DEMME, Jonathan · DONNER, Richard · EASTWOOD, Clint · EMMERICH, Roland · EPHRON, Nora · FARRELLY, Bobby, and Peter Farrelly · HEREK, Stephen · HOWARD, Ron · LEDER, Mimi · LEE, Spike · LEVINSON, Barry · LUCAS, George · LUHRMANN, Baz · MANN, Michael · MARSHALL, Penny · MILLER, George · MINGHELLA, Anthony · NICHOLS, Mike · NOYCE, Phillip · PETERSEN, Wolfgang · POLLACK, Sydney · RAMIS, Harold · REDFORD, Robert · REINER, Rob · REITMAN, Ivan · SCHUMACHER, Joel · SCORSESE, Martin · SCOTT, Ridley · SCOTT, Tony · SHADYAC, Tom · SHELTON, Ron · SODERBERGH, Steven · SONNENFELD, Barry · SPIELBERG, Steven · STONE, Oliver · THOMAS, Betty · VERHOEVEN, Paul · WEIR, Peter · WOO, John · ZEMECKIS, Robert

HELMERS

(Directors)

Only in the last thirty years have directors become the major millionaire players they are today—when just their names attached to a film can be a magnet for financing, A-list actors, and audiences. But a giant ego or a seven- or eight-figure price tag does not an auteur make. Some on the following list are full-service, hands-on filmmakers who develop material from the idea stage and nurture it through production and release, and others are highly paid "shooters" who, like hired guns, are brought on to lend their visual artistry to a film and then move to the next project. This is not necessarily a bad thing. While they may not generate the material they lens, these directors, because they often have developed their signature shooting styles from commercials and music video work, frequently are adept at putting a unique visual stamp on a story. And often these shooters are hired by hands-on producers who micro-manage a project from concept to release. While the following list includes both shooters-for-hire and full-service filmmakers, they all have names that lend a certain cachet to the packaging and marketing process. Although the exact number cannot be accurately determined, many of these helmers are first-dollar gross participants, and a select few (George Lucas and Steven Spielberg top the list) have control over the final cuts of their films. And all have had fairly consistent recent slates of commercial and/or critical successes.

WOODY ALLEN

c/o William Morris Agency
151 El Camino Dr.
Beverly Hills, CA 90212

After more than thirty neurotic years as a director, actor, comic, and even clarinetist, Woody Allen has settled into a once-a-year habit of making movies. He has a newfound cachet as a working actor—in other people's films, like DreamWorks'

WOODY ALLEN (CON'T)

Phone: (310) 859-4000

Fax: (310) 859-4462

animated *Antz*, Douglas McGrath's *Company Man*, and Alfonso Arau's *Picking Up the Pieces*. As a director with legendary credits like *Annie Hall*; *Manhattan*; *Play It Again, Sam*; and *Hannah and Her Sisters*, he still can command megastars to work for scale because he's Woody Allen. Scandal over his former stepdaughter and now wife, Soon-Yi, has never seemed to touch him in Hollywood. (It's more the norm out here.) Though for years he made his films through the now defunct Orion Pictures, Allen has vacillated lately from Miramax to Fine Line (*Celebrity* and *Deconstructing Harry*). On the downside, studios are less likely to handle his films because the bottom line is that though they may be funny to an elitist Zabar's-munching, left-leaning, Ben Shaun–drawings-on-the-wall audience in New York, they don't gross.

MICHAEL BAY

Bay Films

2110 Broadway

Santa Monica, CA 90404

Phone: (310) 829-7799

Fax: (310) 829-7099

Repped by: Creative Artists Agency

Michael Bay leapfrogged from the lucrative but ultimately unheralded world of TV ads (he made the Alexander Hamilton/Aaron Burr "Got Milk" spot) into features with a low-budget effort called *Bad Boys* at Columbia Pictures. The film's $200 million gross worldwide made instant stars out of Will Smith and Martin Lawrence, and turned Bay into a legitimate candidate for jobs on films like *The Rock,* with Sean Connery/Nicolas Cage, and *Armageddon*, starring Bruce Willis/Ben Affleck. All three finished films have thrust Bay and his eponymous production company into the limelight as a gross-participant player in Hollywood's galaxy. He is routinely spotted at parties and on the hot restaurant and bar circuit. And he's automatically considered to direct virtually any action or thriller film in town. Not bad from a guy who signed with Propaganda Management in 1988 as a commercials director on the basis of a lone Donny Osmond music video he directed.

WARREN BEATTY

c/o Creative Artists Agency
9830 Wilshire Blvd.
Beverly Hills, CA 90212
Phone: (310) 288-4545
Fax: (310) 288-4800

No longer the lady-killing bad boy of his youth, Warren Beatty has settled down to fatherhood and wife Annette Bening. However, he does continue to command attention as one of cinema's more provocative and intelligent directors. With his most recent outing, the droll, black political comedy *Bulworth*, Beatty the auteur seemed to have found his groove again. Though not a commercial success, the $35 million pic harkened back to some of the clever political pics of his heyday, from the late '60s through the early '80s, while also representing a bracing reinvigoration of Beatty's own career. The dismal 1994 *Love Affair* and recent press reports chronicling bad blood between Beatty and director Peter Chelsom on the set of the upcoming *Town & Country*, in which he stars with Diane Keaton, should further highlight the argument that if Beatty is going to star in a film, make sure he directs it as well. As for future projects, one closest to Beatty's heart seems to be a long-simmering biopic about Howard Hughes—but he'll have to jump to it, because at least one younger leading man, Leonardo DiCaprio, also is developing a Hughes totem of his own.

LUC BESSON

c/o Seaside Productions
20th Century Fox
10201 West Pico Blvd.
Los Angeles, CA 90035
Phone: (310) 369-1000
Fax: (310) 969-0655
Repped by: International Creative Management

Along with John Woo, Besson, 40, represents the new wave of international action filmmakers who garner acclaim for their skillful direction, darker themes, and stripped-down aesthetic. While nearly all of his films have been huge successes overseas, Besson really didn't gain a global following until his 1990 hit *La Femme Nikita*, which did so well in the U.S. that it was remade into the dreadful 1993 film, *Point of No Return*. He followed with his first Hollywood film, *The Professional*, in 1994, and then his blockbuster sci-fi adventure, *The Fifth Element*, in 1997. While most directors' careers are judged by the success they have had in the U.S. market, Besson sells tickets on a global stage, irrespective of the U.S. box office. While he doesn't need Hollywood's money or influence to get his films made (he has in the past come to the U.S. solely for distribution), studios jump at the chance to work with him. And Besson, who has been called the French Steven Spielberg, is eager to expand his reach in the U.S. He and producing partner, Aimee Peyronnet, recently moved their Seaside Productions from Sony to 20th Century Fox, where they have a first-look deal.

JAMES L. BROOKS

Gracie Films
c/o Sony Pictures Entertainment

James L. Brooks may be the most successful transplant from TV direction to features. A major TV force in the '70s, he created and produced shows like *The Mary Tyler Moore Show*, *Room 222*, *Rhoda*, *Lou Grant*, and *Taxi*. He debuted as a feature director with *Terms of Endearment* in 1983, and has followed it up with

JAMES L. BROOKS (CON'T)

10202 West Washington Blvd.
Poitier Building
Second Floor
Culver City, CA 90232
Phone: (310) 244-4222
Fax: (310) 244-1530
Repped by: International Creative Management

hits *Broadcast News* and *As Good As It Gets*. He stumbled only with *I'll Do Anything*, which started out as a musical, but was quickly shifted to straight comedy. As one of the resident go-to guys on the Sony lot, Brooks gets offers as both director and producer on almost all the major comedies and dramas that Sony produces. Usually, however, he fosters his own creations, like *As Good As It Gets*, which was in development for an eternity and shifted casts several times. But occasionally, he will swing his hefty power base to back a younger director's film like Cameron Crowe's *Jerry Maguire*. Ever the perfectionist, Brooks manicures his films until they're ready to be shown like a freshly polished set of fingernails. He's also outrageously secretive about his future projects and will rarely discuss them outside of his small circle of friends and executives.

TIM BURTON

Tim Burton Productions
1041 North Formosa Ave.
Writers Building
Room 10
Los Angeles, CA 90046
Phone: (323) 850-3100
Fax: (323) 850-3110
Repped by: William Morris Agency

No one is quite sure what twisted thoughts inhabit Tim Burton's psyche, but it's well known that they make money. Burton's rarefied form of dramatic and offbeat storytelling sets him apart from conventional directors and allows him a wide-body DC-10's worth of latitude in making the films that he wants to make, usually for the price he needs. Hence, Burton creates such oddball hits as *Beetle Juice*, *Edward Scissorhands*, *Pee-wee's Big Adventure*, *Ed Wood*, the first *Batman* and *Batman Returns*, and *Mars Attacks*. Though he hasn't directed anything since 1993 he has produced a number of smaller projects like

James and the Giant Peach and *The Nightmare Before Christmas*. And he has *Sleepy Hollow* coming up in 2000. For clothing, he's routinely shrouded in cobweblike forms of black. But how weird is the director who can make even bad boy Johnny Depp seem sane and rational? One friend of his, from their days at the California School of the Arts in the '70s, maintains he would spend hours at a time cogitating while perched on top of his desk like an owl. His acting debut: Cameron Crowe's *Singles*. Burton played Brian.

JAMES CAMERON

Lightstorm Entertainment
919 Santa Monica Blvd.
Santa Monica, CA 90401
Phone: (310) 656-6100
Fax: (310) 656-6102

Following the awesome $2.8 billion box office and multiple Oscar wins stemming from his "art film," *Titanic*, James Cameron suffered a bit of a backlash from the press and even Hollywood at large for his claim to be "King of the World," a title his ego seemed to support. Though he gave up his directing and producing fees during production when *Titanic* began heading wildly over budget, Cameron collected somewhere near $110 million from his gross participation on the film. He's always been known as a budget-buster (his *True Lies* was reportedly the first film to cross the $100 million mark, and *Titanic* easily passed $200 million), but while each film ups the ante, except for *The Abyss,* he has managed to deliver an almost incomparable string of hits, including *Terminator*, *Aliens*, *True Lies*, *Terminator 2: Judgment Day*, and *Titanic*. Along with George Lucas, Cameron is hailed as a visionary of film special effects—he's also a triple threat, usually writing, directing, and producing the films he makes. Based at Fox, Cameron owes the studio another film. He'll most likely produce *Planet of the Apes*, a *True Lies* sequel, and possibly *Terminator 3*, but his next directorial outing has yet to materialize.

JOEL COEN AND ETHAN COEN

c/o United Talent Agency
9560 Wilshire Blvd.
Beverly Hills, CA 90212
Phone: (310) 273-6700
Fax: (310) 247-1111

This director-producer brother act gets at least partial credit (or blame, depending on your viewpoint) for the explosion in American independent filmmaking since the '80s. Starting in 1984 with the stylishly gruesome noir thriller *Blood Simple*, the duo have brought their unique voice to such stalwart genres as the domestic farce (*Raising Arizona*), the gangland mob pic (*Miller's Crossing*), and the police procedural (*Fargo*). The Coens demonstrate considerably more versatility and affection for their characters than latter-day indie icons Quentin Tarantino and Danny Boyle. While there have been box office disappointments along the way (i.e., *Hudsucker Proxy* and *The Big Lebowski*), the brothers maintain their rarefied status as filmmakers who make the movies they want to and, with some consistency, achieve commercial success.

CHRIS COLUMBUS

1492 Pictures

A first-dollar gross player after directing such hits as *Home Alone*, *Home Alone 2,* and *Mrs. Doubtfire*, Chris Columbus sprinkled that success with such misfires as *Only the Lonely* and *Nine Months*. Though 20th Century Fox signed

CHRIS COLUMBUS (CON'T)

c/o 20th Century Fox
10201 West Pico Blvd.
Building 86
Los Angeles, CA 90035
Phone: (310) 369-2368
Fax: (310) 369-4743
Repped by:
Creative Artists Agency

Columbus and his 1492 Pictures to two consecutive first-look deals, for which the hyphenate was to write, produce, and direct films, Columbus has not directed a film for the studio since 1995's *Nine Months*. (Columbus and 1492 partners Michael Barnathan and Mark Radcliffe produced 1996's *Jingle All the Way*.) Despite a couple dozen projects in development at Fox, Columbus instead chose to make his next outing in 1998 for Sony, with the Susan Sarandon/Julia Roberts weepy, *Stepmom*; he followed it with the $100 million-plus Robin Williams–starrer, *Bicentennial Man*, a co-production between Disney and Sony. Columbus and his 1492 mates are, however, producing the upcoming live-action/stop-motion animation feature, *Monkeybone*, starring Brendan Fraser, under Henry Selick's helm, for Fox Animation Studios.

FRANCIS FORD COPPOLA

American Zoetrope
916 Kearny St.
San Francisco, CA 94133
Phone: (415) 788-7500
Fax: (415) 989-7910
Repped by: International
Creative Management

The Oscar-winning director of *The Godfather* trilogy, *Apocolypse Now*, and *The Conversation* has lately been reduced to director-for-hire work on lackluster programmers such as *Jack* (1996) and *The Rainmaker* (1997) while pursuing other interests, including publishing, winemaking, and litigation. But given the roller-coaster nature of Coppola's nearly four-decade-long career, few in Hollywood are betting against the possibility he'll make yet another comeback. After his American Zoetrope sought bankruptcy protection twice in five years, he won a $20 million decision against Warner Bros. over his aborted live-action *Pinocchio* feature. In 1998, Coppola announced ambitious plans for the latest incarnation of Zoetrope, including the financing and distribution of several low-budget pics. The company's first projects included *The Virgin Suicides*, the feature directorial debut of Coppola's daughter, Sofia; *The Florentine*, starring Michael Madsen and Chris Penn; and Agnieszka Holland's *The Third Miracle*, starring Ed Harris and Anne Heche.

While still at UCLA Film School, Coppola got his start as the director of the 1961 soft-core porn pic *Tonight for Sure* before hooking up with B-movie impresario Roger Corman, for whom he helmed the 1963 horror pic *Dementia 13*. That was followed three years later by *You're a Big Boy Now* and five years later by the failed screen musical *Finian's Rainbow*. In 1969, Coppola set up his San Francisco–based American Zoetrope, bringing in none other than future *Star Wars* creator George Lucas as his second-in-command. The company produced Lucas's economical sci-fier *THX 1138*. Coppola won an Adapted Screenplay Oscar for 1970's *Patton*; his 1972 *The Godfather* and its 1974 sequel won Academy Awards for Best Picture. The same year (1974) saw the release of the finely observed character study *The Conversation*.

WES CRAVEN

c/o Wes Craven Films

While this former English teacher made his bones in the lowbrow horror genre, his *A Nightmare on Elm Street* and his collaboration with writer Kevin Williamson on the *Scream* series—

WES CRAVEN (CON'T)

11846 Ventura Blvd.
Suite 208
Studio City, CA 91604
Phone: (818) 752-0197
Fax: (818) 752-1789
Repped by: International Creative Management

two of the most successful film franchises in history—proved that Craven, at fifty-nine, had more up top than exploitation. Each of these franchises served not only to raise Craven's stature in the industry, but also helped elevate their distributors (New Line Cinema and Dimension Films, respectively) from genre labels to mainstream players.

The nearly billion-dollar box office of his horror films has made Craven a branded name in the genre business, and has expanded his career opportunities. Though he most likely will return to direct the third *Scream* film, his new clout allowed him to take the helm recently of an atypical project, *50 Violins*, a biopic of inner-city music teacher Roberta Guispari-Tzavaras, starring Meryl Streep.

CAMERON CROWE

c/o Vinyl Films
1663 Euclid St.
Santa Monica, CA 90404
Phone: (310) 234-7655
Fax: (310) 234-7656
Repped by:
Creative Artists Agency

After coaxing an Oscar-nominated comedic performance out of Tom Cruise on the $154 million domestic grosser *Jerry Maguire*, writer-director-producer Crowe inked a three-year first-look pact with DreamWorks that ends in mid-2000. In 1999, Crowe began work on an as yet untitled semi-biographical drama about a teenage rock journalist in the '70s. The director actually wrote for *Rolling Stone* at the tender age of 16, before scripting 1982's seminal high school sex comedy *Fast Times at Ridgemont High*. Now a card-carrying member of the Woody Allen school of stealth production, Crowe insists on keeping his story lines under wraps for as long as possible—even from his supporting players. This much is known, however: Once lengthy pre-production rehearsals begin, Crowe employs a highly collaborative process he likens to that of Brit helmer Mike Leigh.

FRANK DARABONT

c/o William Morris Agency
151 El Camino Dr.
Beverly Hills, CA 90212
Phone: (310) 859-4000
Fax: (310) 859-4462

Writer-director Frank Darabont broke into the big leagues with his ambitious directorial 1994 debut, *The Shawshank Redemption*. In order to direct the film, Darabont reportedly turned down the $2.4 million that Castle Rock Entertainment offered solely for his screenplay adaptation of Stephen King's novella *Rita Hayworth and Shawshank Redemption*, with the chance to direct another film. Darabont held out, and accepted $750,000 to write and direct the pic, which went on to garner seven Oscar nominations, including Best Picture and Best Adapted Screenplay. Four years after *Shawshank* was released, as the first of a new two-picture deal with Castle Rock, Darabont mounted his sophomore outing, *The Green Mile* (1999), another period prison film adapted from King's fiction—in this case from the collection of short stories *The Night Shift*. *Green Mile* followed Darabont's uncredited rewrite of Steven Spielberg's *Saving Private Ryan*, which starred Tom Hanks (he starred in both films). The second film in his Castle Rock pact is *The Bijou*, a Capra-esque romantic comedy set against the blacklist of the 1950s.

Written by Darabont's high school buddy Michael Sloane, *Bijou* serves as Darabont's first directing effort from a script that he did not write.

JAN DE BONT

Blue Tulip Productions
1658 10th St.
Santa Monica, CA 90404
Phone: (310) 752-7900
Fax: (310) 752-7920
Repped by:
The Gersh Agency

Following the 1994 breakaway hit *Speed*, his helming debut, cinematographer Jan de Bont emerged as one of the premier action directors in Hollywood, commanding nearly $3 million for his next film, *Twister*, another big summer hit. But when he returned to Fox to direct the sequel to *Speed*, whatever momentum he had was soon drowned in a sea of red ink and bad notices. *Speed 2: Cruise Control* ended up with an estimated $150 million price tag but brought in only $48.6 million domestically. His production company, Blue Tulip Prods., has a first-look deal with Fox, for which De Bont has not directed a film since *Speed 2*. This has put De Bont on the defensive, having to overcome a perception that he is an adept "shooter" who cannot control budgets or direct actors. Fox, which scuttled his event pic *Ghost Riders in the Sky* over budget and script concerns, allowed him to go to DreamWorks to helm *The Haunting*. In return, the studio expects to get his next film, which could be a scaled-back version of *Ghost Riders*. Because of his involvement with *The Haunting*, De Bont took his name out of the director slot for the sci-fi thriller *Minority Report* for Fox, a project that Steven Spielberg will direct and Tom Cruise will star in.

JONATHAN DEMME

Clinica Estetico
127 West 24th St.
New York, NY 10011
Phone: (212) 807-6800
Fax: (212) 807-6830
Repped by:
Creative Artists Agency

One of Hollywood's critically acclaimed directors for such films as *Philadelphia*, *Silence of the Lambs*, *Beloved*, *Married to the Mob*, *Stop Making Sense*, *Swimming to Cambodia*, *Swing Shift*, and *Something Wild*, Jonathan Demme took a circuitous route to build his career. He worked as an actor, publicist, film salesman, unit publicist (for Roger Corman), usher, kennel worker, hospital attendant, and freelance film reviewer before directing his first film, *Caged Heat*, for Corman in 1974. Now with an Oscar in tow for directing *Silence of the Lambs*, Demme picks and chooses carefully with his Gotham/L.A. Clinica Estetico production company in the Universal Pictures fold. He likes to back young directors and will often lend his name to "present" their films (*Ulee's Gold*, *Six Ways to Sunday*), immediately providing weight. The progressive director also jumps on political bandwagons, such as the fight in the early '90s to re-establish Jean-Bertrand Aristide in power in Haiti. Demme lashed out at the Haitian regime at a rally in Central Park that drew more than 100,000. After being stung by charges of homophobia for *Silence of the Lambs*, he quieted critics with the award-winning film about AIDS patients' rights, *Philadelphia*.

RICHARD DONNER

Donner/Shuler-Donner
Productions
c/o Warner Bros.

If you called Richard Donner one of Hollywood's grossest directors, it wouldn't be an insult. Only a few major directors participate in first-dollar gross returns. Donner is one of them. He made so much with Mel Gibson and Danny

RICHARD DONNER (CON'T)

4000 Warner Blvd.
Building 102
Burbank, CA 91522
Phone: (818) 954-3961
Fax: (818) 954-4908
Repped by: William Morris Agency & Artists Management Group

Glover on *Lethal Weapon 4* that Warner Bros. ultimately enjoyed only minimal profits on the film, which grossed more than $130 million domestically. Donner won't even consider directing anything these days unless he's a gross player. And invariably, since high-priced action films are his forte, he takes home a considerable chunk of change. He usually produces with his wife, Lauren Shuler-Donner, films like the *Free Willy* franchise. A TV director in the '60s and '70s on such shows as *The Twilight Zone*, *The Fugitive*, and *The Man from U.N.C.L.E.*, his feature credits include all four *Lethal Weapon* films, *Superman*, *The Omen*, *Maverick*, *Scrooged*, *Conspiracy Theory*, and *Ladyhawke*, among others. The grandson of a movie theater owner, Donner is one of the regular lunch patrons of the Warner Bros. commissary, often spotted with Gibson.

CLINT EASTWOOD

Malpaso Productions
c/o Warner Bros.
4000 Warner Blvd.
Building 81
First Floor
Burbank, CA 91522
Phone: (818) 954-3367
Fax: (818) 954-4803
Repped by:
William Morris Agency

Did he make five hit films, or was it six? In all the confusion, Hollywood kinda lost track. Eastwood has actually directed twenty feature films in Hollywood and produced even more under his Malpaso banner. Dirty Harry notwithstanding, Eastwood has proven himself year after year as an actor (*Dirty Harry* franchise, *Every Which Way but Loose* franchise, *In the Line of Fire*, *Play Misty for Me*) and as a director with films such as *Unforgiven*, *The Bridges of Madison County*, and *The Eiger Sanction*. Former Warner co-chairs Bob Daly and Terry Semel worshipped at the Eastwood altar and would greenlight virtually anything the star seriously developed. Lately, he's suffered underachievers with *Midnight in the Garden of Good and Evil*, *Absolute Power*, and *True Crime*. But Warner doesn't care. He's still Clint. Next on his agenda is a film that he may personally understand, *Space Cowboys*. It's about a group of astronauts forced to go on a dangerous space mission. Like Clint, they're all past Social Security age.

ROLAND EMMERICH

Centropolis Entertainment
c/o Sony Pictures
10202 West Washington Blvd.
Astaire Building
Third Floor
Culver City, CA 90232
Phone: (310) 244-4300
Fax: (310) 244-4360
Repped by:
Creative Artists Agency

Roland Emmerich began his career as a geeky film student after seeing Erich van Daniken's *Chariots of the Gods?* in 1974. That's where he got the idea for *Stargate*. With partner Dean Devlin, whom he met when Devlin was an actor in his 1990 West German film *Moon 44*, he has since moved on to pricier fare with *Independence Day*, which became an international phenomenon, and *Godzilla*, which didn't. After *ID* and its $507 million gross, the pair were able to dictate the terms of a huge overall deal with Sony Pictures. After *Godzilla*, which grossed $250 million worldwide but barely broke even with a sizable yawn from a Godzilla-saturated public, it looked to the industry like one of the biggest joke deals ever. Still, Sony seems keen on the pair, who operate under the Centropolis Entertainment banner and have films out like *The Thirteenth Floor*. Their names have been bandied about for other high-profile sequels, like the James Bond feature that Sony wanted to steal from MGM/UA, as well as the *Spiderman* hopeful.

NORA EPHRON

c/o William Morris Agency
151 El Camino Dr.
Beverly Hills, CA 90212
Phone: (310) 859-4000
Fax: (310) 859-4462

Nora Ephron started out as a fresh-scrubbed cub reporter for the *New York Post* in 1963. It wasn't until 1983 that she saw her first screenplay credit (with writer Alice Arlen) on the big screen with *Silkwood*. Three more screenplays later (*Heartburn*, *When Harry Met Sally . . .*, *Cookie*), Ephron directed and wrote (with her sister Delia) the unspectacular *This Is My Life*. She jumped to A-list director status with 1993's *Sleepless in Seattle*, featuring an acting duo of Tom Hanks and Meg Ryan (as well as a story) she revisited five years later in *You've Got Mail*. In between, she churned out the severely disappointing *Mixed Nuts* and the surprise John Travolta hit *Michael*. Though she's not a gross player in the traditional sense, Ephron, as one of the premier women directors in Hollywood, can effectively convince most of the studios around town to make her films. She's particularly tight with Warner Bros. and Columbia. Married to journo and screenwriter Nick Pileggi.

BOBBY FARRELLY AND PETER FARRELLY

Conundrum Entertainment

After witnessing the incredible, $328 million worldwide success of *There's Something About Mary*, the industry learned what Bobby and Peter Farrelly have known for some time: Comedy is serious business. *Mary* was just the latest, and most successful, entry on their résumé, which includes the signature farces *Dumb and Dumber* and *Kingpin*. Described by Fox senior exec Tom Rothman as "high masters of low art," the Farrellys now stand as arbiters of

BOBBY FARRELLY AND PETER FARRELLY (CON'T)
1410 Second St.
Santa Monica, CA 90401
Phone: (310) 458-3338
Fax: (310) 458-1048
Repped by:
Creative Artists Agency

(albeit oxymoronic) smart, low-brow comedy (their credo being "We try to go to a place where people don't expect us to go") that every studio is scrambling to copy (note Warner Bros.' lame attempt with *Lost and Found*, starring David Spade). The town is now their oyster. Luckily, Fox signed them to a multi-year production pact before the success of *Mary*, a move that is already paying off. The Farrellys' follow-up is *Me, Myself and Irene*, starring Jim Carrey.

STEPHEN HEREK

Mud Pony Productions
500 South Buena Vista St.
Animation Building
Suite 2E-13
Burbank, CA 91521-1756
Phone: (818) 848-4011
Fax: (818) 848-5236
Repped by: Endeavor Agency

Stephen Herek is what *Variety* calls one of its $1 billion directors because his films—which include *101 Dalmatians*, *Holy Man*, *Mr. Holland's Opus*, *The Mighty Ducks*, *Three Musketeers*, *Don't Tell Mom the Babysitter's Dead*, *Bill and Ted's Excellent Adventure*, and *Critters*—have grossed that much domestically. So when he attaches himself to a film, it usually carries some industry weight. He has a sweet overall deal with Disney, but it's not exclusive. Next up will likely be *102 Dalmatians* for Disney. Though his films read like a Disney manifesto, it always surprises people to find out that he started with Roger Corman's New World Pictures as a film editor.

RON HOWARD

Imagine Entertainment

He ain't Opie anymore. At least that's what his producing partner Brian Grazer will insist about Ron Howard, who has directed more than a

RON HOWARD (CON'T)
9465 Wilshire Blvd.
Seventh Floor
Beverly Hills, CA 90212
Phone: (310) 858-2000
Fax: (310) 858-2020
Repped by:
Creative Artists Agency

dozen high-profile, A-list star-filled films like *Apollo 13*, *Ransom*, *EdTV*, *Far and Away*, *Backdraft*, *Parenthood*, *Cocoon*, *Night Shift*, and *Splash*. A former sitcom fave on *The Andy Griffith Show* and *Happy Days*, Howard decided as an adult he was much happier behind the camera. Now, he and Grazer have built Imagine Entertainment into perhaps the most successful and most sought-after film production company in Hollywood. Though theoretically Imagine has to run potential films by its parent company Universal, the truth is that Howard and Grazer can make anything they want, and Universal happily says yes.

MIMI LEDER

c/o DreamWorks SKG
100 Universal City Plaza
Building 477
Universal City, CA 91608
Phone: (818) 733-7000
Fax: (818) 509-1433
Repped by:
Creative Artists Agency

The Emmy Award–winning director and co-exec producer of NBC's *ER* first turned her sights to the big screen on DreamWorks' moderately successful debut release *The Peacemaker*. But it was her second feature, Paramount and DreamWorks' $350 million global hit *Deep Impact*, that launched her feature career into the stratosphere. While she eschews the label "woman director," *Impact*'s success was attributed in part to Leder's ability to bring emotional force to the shopworn disaster genre. Not content to be typecast as a distaff hardware helmer, Leder has signed on to direct a number of smaller pics, including Universal's family drama *Still Life* and, along with her brother Reuben, *Sentimental Journey*, a holocaust tale based on the true story of her parents.

SPIKE LEE

40 Acres & A Mule Filmworks, Inc.
124 DeKalb Avenue
Brooklyn, NY 11217
Phone: (718) 624-3703
Fax: (718) 624-2008
Repped by: International Creative Management

Spike Lee's gotta have it. The problem is that he's not sure what to do with it. The most outspoken man in Hollywood, black or otherwise, Lee makes movies and moves based largely on his emotional complaint that the industry is inherently racist. Hence, the antebellum monicker of his production company, 40 Acres & A Mule. His films are rarely hits, though some of them are earners like *He Got Game* and *Do the Right Thing*. They're invariably critically well-received, but critics still pine for his indie days of such films as *She's Gotta Have It*. And Spike can usually convince studios to see things his way for a budget. *Malcolm X* skyrocketed over its original budget, but *He Got Game* clocked in under $29 million and proved profitable. He's been through deals at Columbia and Universal and now Disney. Outside of filmmaking, Lee may be better known for his courtside antics at New York Knicks games. His long-running feud (in jest?) with Indiana Pacer Reggie Miller has been the stuff that basketball dreams are made of.

BARRY LEVINSON

c/o Baltimore / Spring Creek Pictures
4000 Warner Blvd.
Building 133
Room 208
Burbank, CA 91522
Phone: (818) 954-2210
Fax: (818) 954-2693

Since 1982, when he served up his semi-autobiographical feature debut *Diner*, this Baltimore-born college dropout has alternated between critically acclaimed blockbusters such as *Good Morning, Vietnam* and *Rain Man* and more personal—if sometimes less financially rewarding—semi-autobiographical works like *Avalon* and *Liberty Heights*. The onetime standup comic got his first big break as a writer-performer on *The Carol Burnett Show*

BARRY LEVINSON (CON'T)

Repped by: Artists Management Group

in the mid-'70s and later co-wrote Mel Brooks's parody classics *High Anxiety* and *Silent Movie*. Despite several high-profile clunkers, including *Toys* and *Sphere*, Levinson remains firmly on Hollywood's A-list. He has a reputation for going with his gut on the set, shunning rehearsals and listening to suggestions from his stars. Also a prolific producer, Levinson teamed up in 1998 with Paula Weinstein to form the Warner Bros.–based Baltimore/ Spring Creek Prods., whose credits include *Analyze This*. Levinson was recently reunited with longtime producing partner Mark Johnson on the Irish comedy *An Everlasting Piece*. Not forgetting his small-screen roots, the filmmaker also had success with the long-running drama series *Homicide: Life on the Street*.

GEORGE LUCAS

Lucasfilm, Ltd.
P.O. Box 2009
San Raphael, CA 94912
Phone: (415) 662-1800
Fax: (415) 444-8240

In the twenty-two years since his last directorial outing *(Star Wars)* George Lucas has lived in his Northern California compound as a billionaire semi-recluse, but in 1999 you couldn't get away from him. The reason of course was the release of his long-in-the-works *Star Wars: Episode I—The Phantom Menace*, the first of three prequels in the *Star Wars* series.

Suspicious and dismissive of the Hollywood studio system, Lucas—who owns the copyrights, and thus all ancillary rights, to all three of the original *Star Wars* films—funded the $125 million *Phantom Menace* out of his own pocket, hiring Fox (for a reported 7 percent fee) to distribute the film around the world. Lucas will use the massive receipts from *Phantom Menace* to fund the next two prequels, which he likely will direct and which he will shoot entirely in a digital format. Lucas, a single father of three adopted kids, runs an international multimedia conglomerate, boasting Lucasfilm and its various divisions, which include special effects house Industrial Light & Magic; and Skywalker Sound, which provides post-production sound technology for the film industry and serves as a hi-tech mixing studio for the music industry. LucasArts develops and produces CD-ROM games (including *Rebel Assault*) and interactive learning games for children.

BAZ LUHRMANN

c/o Bazmark Inc.
2 Darley St.
Darlinghurst, Sydney, NSW
Australia 2010
Phone: 011-6129-361-6668
Fax: 011-6129-361-6667
Repped by: International Creative Management

Though he has just two film credits under his belt, Luhrmann has emerged as one of the most important filmmakers on today's global stage. The Aussie is regarded as in the vanguard not only of the recent wave of Australian filmmakers who have made a mark in Hollywood and at home, including P. J. Hogan (*My Best Friend's Wedding*) and Stephan Elliott (*Adventures of Priscilla, Queen of the Desert*), but also of a new generation of "multi-media" artists. His 1996 rendition of *William Shakespeare's Romeo + Juliet* launched the superstar careers of Leonardo DiCaprio and Claire Danes, and exposed the sophistication and box office viability of the young female audience to which Hollywood now panders shamelessly. Luhrmann has his hands in music, fashion, stage shows, and location-based entertainment. A friend of the

Murdoch family, he has a long-term, wide-reaching, multi-year deal with Rupert Murdoch–owned 20th Century Fox, for which he next directs a musical set at the end of the last millennium.

MICHAEL MANN

c/o Creative Artists Agency
9830 Wilshire Blvd.
Beverly Hills, CA 90212
Phone: (310) 288-4545
Fax: (310) 288-4800

Chicago-born Michael Mann, who cut his teeth writing for such TV cop shows as *Starsky and Hutch* and *Vega$* before executive producing *Miami Vice*, became one of Hollywood's leading film directors and writers in the late '80s and '90s. During this time he has helmed such films as the cool heist pic *Thief* (his feature debut in 1981), the psychological thriller *Manhunter* (1986), a revisionist adaptation of *The Last of the Mohicans* (1992), and the crime drama *Heat* (1995), which marked the first-time onscreen pairing of Robert De Niro and Al Pacino. Mann, who studied at London Film School, also has been lauded for his detailed, lively screenplays and complex, visually textured direction, all of which attracts top talent. Mann's next release will be Disney's still-untitled tobacco industry exposé, starring Pacino. He also is developing a Howard Hughes biopic to star Leonardo DiCaprio.

PENNY MARSHALL

Parkway Productions
c/o Universal Pictures

Though her look and that accent invariably reek of Laverne de Fazio, Penny Marshall has carved herself a career as a female director who gets it. Her showbiz older brother, Garry Marshall,

PENNY MARSHALL (CON'T)

100 Universal City Plaza
Bungalow 105
Universal City, CA 91608
Phone: (818) 777-7107
Fax: (818) 866-4616
Repped by: William Morris Agency

helped develop her keen wit and eye. So it's easy to see why she could segue from acting on *The Odd Couple* and *Laverne and Shirley* to feature directing of such hits as *Big*, *A League of Their Own*, *Awakenings*, and *The Preacher's Wife*, despite the latter's poor box office performance. As one of a select few women who can generate a green light with interest, Marshall chooses her battles carefully, directing a film only once every two years. She was married to Rob Reiner; their daughter, Tracy, later became an actress and appeared in some of her mom's films.

GEORGE MILLER

9300 Wilshire Blvd.
Beverly Hills, CA 90212
Phone: (310) 278-8070
Fax: (310) 278-6058
Repped by: The Irv Schecter Company

After the media pork roast of *Babe: Pig in the City* in 1998, George Miller's luster was somewhat dimmed. Until then, the Aussie director was considered money in the bank with such films as the *Mad Max* franchise and the original *Babe*, which he wrote, produced, and Chris Noonan directed. He also enjoyed success with *Witches of Eastwick* and *Lorenzo's Oil*. But *Babe 2* went so far over budget and was so widely perceived as too dark for kids that Universal was forced to can then president Casey Silver. Still, Miller is on the A-list of directors in town and can always find a decent paycheck if he wants it. He studied medicine at the New South Wales Medical School before turning to film under fellow Australian director Phillip Noyce. In fact, the only reason Miller was able to finish *Mad Max*, the first of the cult wasteland series, was that he paid the rent with his tiny practice as a physician.

ANTHONY MINGHELLA

c/o William Morris Agency
151 El Camino Dr.
Beverly Hills, CA 90212
Phone: (310) 859-4000
Fax: (310) 859-4462

Before *The English Patient*, Anthony Minghella had directed only two pictures, but *Patient*'s nine Oscar wins, including Best Director and Best Picture, helped catapult the Brit-raised son of Italian parents onto the A-list of Hollywood writer/directors. He first garnered attention writing for the London stage, such legit works as *Made in Bangkok*, which was dubbed best play of 1986 by the London theater critics. Minghella then segued to writing for TV, where he penned episodes of the well-regarded English mystery series *Inspector Morse*. Moving on to directing, in 1990 he filmed a short, *Living with Dinosaurs*, for Jim Henson Productions and made his feature debut directing the 1991 comedy-fantasy *Truly, Madly, Deeply*. Minghella's first Hollywood film, 1993's *Mr. Wonderful*, starred Matt Dillon and Annabella Sciorra. But this foundation of experience could not prepare Minghella for the success that would befall him following his 1996 adaptation of Michael Ondaatje's novel *The English Patient*, starring Ralph Fiennes and Kristin Scott Thomas. Stars now clamor to work with him and studios will spend big money for his services. United Artists paid $1.25 million for the rights to Charles Frazier's *Cold Mountain* as a potential follow-up to Minghella's latest, *The Talented Mr. Ripley*, which stars Matt Damon and Gwyneth Paltrow.

MIKE NICHOLS

9830 Wilshire Blvd.

Mike Nichols is known as an actors' director because he once was a struggling thesp with comedy partner Elaine May. Nichols stopped his

MIKE NICHOLS (CON'T)

Beverly Hills, CA 90212

Phone: (310) 288-4545

Fax: (310) 288-4800

Repped by: Creative Artists Agency

shtick with May in 1961, moving on to direct theater on Broadway (*Barefoot in the Park* and *The Odd Couple*) and generation-defining films (*Who's Afraid of Virginia Woolf?* and *The Graduate*). These days, he can name the film and studios come begging. Though they aren't always box office bonanzas, Nichols's films are high-profile and draw top-drawer names: *Primary Colors*, *The Birdcage*, *Wolf*, *Regarding Henry*, *Working Girl*, *Postcards from the Edge*, *Heartburn*, and *Silkwood*. His handiwork was honored by the Film Society of Lincoln Center in 1999. Ever the New Yorker, Nichols is married to TV journalist Diane Sawyer, and the couple is considered a must-invite for any industry cocktailer or party.

PHILLIP NOYCE

Rumbalara Films

7001 Melrose Ave.

Los Angeles, CA 90038

Phone: (323) 936-4436

Fax: (323) 936-4913

Repped by: Endeavor Agency

Australian writer-director Noyce had turned out a number of award-winning films and TV projects down under before making a splash in Hollywood with his economical 1989 seafaring thriller *Dead Calm*. After an unimpressive American debut (Rutger Hauer–starrer *Blind Fury*) Noyce began a largely successful six-year run with Paramount Pictures. He helmed the second installment of Paramount's Jack Ryan franchise, *Patriot Games* (1992), based on the Tom Clancy bestseller; the muddled Sharon Stone sex thriller *Sliver* (1993); Par's *Patriot Games* follow-up *Clear and Present Danger*, which scored big at the box office in 1994; and Par's moderately successful big-screen version of *The Saint* (1997). But in 1997, frustrated by Paramount's apparent unwillingness to back a remake of the Graham Greene novel *The Quiet American* at the budget level he felt it warranted, Noyce inked a two-year deal for his Rumbalara Films production company at ill-fated PolyGram Films. In 1998 he directed Universal's *The Bone Collector*, starring Denzel Washington and Angelina Jolie. Noyce, an iconoclast and a consummate world traveler, is known for his restless curiosity and intellectual energy.

WOLFGANG PETERSEN

Radiant Productions
914 Montana Ave.
Second Floor
Santa Monica, CA 90403
Phone: (310) 656-1400
Fax: (310) 656-1408
Repped by:
Creative Artists Agency

German-born Wolfgang Petersen became an overnight sensation at age forty when he was the first director nominated for an Oscar for a German film with *Das Boot*. Though he followed the U-boat thriller with *The NeverEnding Story*, *Enemy Mine*, and *Shattered*, he didn't really find financial heat again until *In the Line of Fire* with Clint Eastwood and John Malkovich in 1993. He inadvertently inherited the action director mantle, handling *Outbreak* and then the outrageously successful *Air Force One*. His name is usually bandied as a potential for any serious action thriller, and he does take a small piece of the gross.

SYDNEY POLLACK

Mirage Enterprises
c/o Sony Pictures
10202 West Washington Blvd.

He grew up in the country environs of South Bend, Ind., but Sydney Pollack is assiduously urban in the subject matter of his films like *The Firm*; *Havana*; *Sabrina*; *Tootsie*; *Absence of Malice*; *The Way We Were*; *They Shoot Horses,*

SYDNEY POLLACK (CON'T)

Lean Building
Suite 119
Culver City, CA 90232
Phone: (310) 244-2044
Fax: (310) 244-0044
Repped by:
Artists Management Agency

Don't They?; and *This Property Is Condemned.* As an actor, he also comes off as the quintessential city-dweller in such films as *Husbands and Wives*, *A Civil Action*, *The Player*, and even his own *Tootsie*, opposite Dustin Hoffman. His thespian talents date back to early study with New York teacher Sanford Meisner in the '50s. Pollack has an overall production deal with Sony Pictures, largely because Sony chairman John Calley wanted a good friend at the studio. There had been a rumor that the pair might team up with outside financing in a production deal of their own. Both denied it. But Pollack has not been tremendously productive in his deal, with only *Random Hearts* to show for it. Meanwhile, his Mirage Enterprises yields him producer or executive producer credit on such films as *Sliding Doors*; *Sense and Sensibility*; *Searching for Bobby Fischer*; *Leaving Normal*; *The Fabulous Baker Boys*; *Bright Lights, Big City*; and *Dead Again.* Last out for the director was *Random Hearts* for Columbia. Now, he's looking for a new gig.

HAROLD RAMIS

Ocean Pictures
c/o 20th Century Fox
10201 West Pico Blvd.
Building 12
Los Angeles, CA 90035

Harold Ramis's career got a gigantic shot in the arm in 1999 with the surprise blockbuster success of the Billy Crystal/Robert DeNiro *Analyze This*—which put the actors, particularly Crystal, and director back in the big leagues. With the film's long-lasting box office appeal (nearly ten weeks in the top 10), Ramis is once again firmly established as one of the town's premier comedy directors. In fact, Warner

HAROLD RAMIS (CON'T)

Phone: (310) 369-0093

Fax: (310) 369-7742

Repped by:

Creative Artists Agency

Bros. is looking to re-team Ramis and his stars in either a sequel or another similar concept. Ramis's status as an A-list writer-director should have been secure, with writing credits on such pics as *National Lampoon's Animal House*, *Meatballs*, and *Stripes*, and a directing stint with *Caddyshack*. But after the fizzle of *Ghostbusters 2* (which he wrote) and a string of acting stints in the late '80s (*Baby Boom*, *Stealing Home*), Hollywood cooled to Ramis as a filmmaker. While he returned to the director's chair in 1993 with the surprise hit *Groundhog Day*, starring Bill Murray, his follow-ups—*Stuart Saves His Family* and *Multiplicity*—knocked him back a few steps, until *Analyze This*, which had Billy Crystal playing shrink to mob boss Robert De Niro. Though Ramis and DreamWorks agreed to part company on the Tim Allen–starrer *Galaxy Quest* in 1999, Ramis is fielding numerous offers to direct as well as developing his own projects under his Fox-based Ocean Pictures production banner, which he runs with Trevor Albert.

ROBERT REDFORD

c/o Wildwood Enterprises

1101 Montana Ave.

Suite E

Santa Monica, CA 90403

Perhaps the ultimate multi-hyphenate, Redford not only has earned artistic and commercial success as an actor, writer, producer, and director, he's also helped foster emerging talent as the founder of the Sundance Institute and its well-known festival offshoot. The Southern California–born thesp took his first giant step as an actor in the 1963 Broadway hit *Barefoot in the Park*, but his feature career didn't reach full gal-

ROBERT REDFORD (CON'T)

Phone: (310) 395-5155

Fax: (310) 395-3975

Repped by: Creative Artists Agency

lop until the 1969 Western comedy *Butch Cassidy and the Sundance Kid*. Redford made his directing debut on critics' fave *Ordinary People*, released in 1980—the same year Sundance was born. Redford is still hotly sought after as an actor on studio pics, which he sandwiches between carefully chosen helming projects. A measure of his studio clout: Disney's $3 million bid for the rights to Nicholas Evans's incomplete first novel *The Horse Whisperer*, which became the first film Redford both starred in and directed. Meanwhile, Sundance, now the premier U.S. festival and a hot market for specialized film, has expanded its reach into cable TV and theatrical exhibition.

ROB REINER

Castle Rock Entertainment

335 North Maple Dr.

Suite 135

Beverly Hills, CA 90210

Phone: (310) 285-2300

Fax: (310) 285-2345

Repped by: International Creative Management

Still occasionally termed "Meathead" after his *All in the Family* days, Rob Reiner has long since graduated to directing A-list films like *A Few Good Men*, *Princess Bride*, *When Harry Met Sally . . .*, *Misery*, *The American President*, and *Ghosts of Mississippi*. Through Castle Rock, which he helped co-found a decade ago, Reiner automatically has a green light for any film he wishes to make. Strangely enough, this son of Carl Reiner only rarely makes comedies like *When Harry Met Sally. . . .* He prefers more serious-toned themes of civil rights–era racism, military aggression, and political hanky-panky. Reiner saves the laughs for his cameo appearances in films of his friends like Nora Ephron, Woody Allen, Danny DeVito, and Mike Nichols.

IVAN REITMAN

Montecito Picture Company
1482 East Valley Road
Suite 477
Montecito, CA 93108
Phone: (805) 565-8590
Fax: (805) 565-8661
Repped by:
Creative Artists Agency

Ivan Reitman is one of the out-and-out best in comedy as director and producer. He produced *Animal House*, directed *Meatballs*, and produced and directed *Twins* and *Ghostbusters*. His last production deal at Universal was so lucrative, he was able to build an altogether separate building on the Universal lot that is now inhabited by Gary Ross's and Will Smith's companies. Now, however, Reitman's star may be dimming a bit. His new five-year Montecito deal with Tom Pollock had a rocky start. Originally, it was with Polygram before the company was sold to Universal. Now, nobody knows where it's going to land. His last film was *Six Days, Seven Nights*, which didn't make squat in the U.S., but did fine in Europe and Asia.

JOEL SCHUMACHER

Joel Schumacher Productions
c/o Warner Bros.
4000 Warner Blvd.
Building 81
Room 207
Burbank, CA 91522
Phone: (818) 954-2508
Fax: (818) 954-2509
Repped by:
Creative Artists Agency

Schumacher developed a youthful following in the '80s with his Brat Pack trilogy *St. Elmo's Fire*, *Flatliners*, and *The Lost Boys*, but it was the middle-aged urban stress-out pic *Falling Down* that put him in Hollywood's big leagues. After that, he racked up an impressive string of hits, including the John Grisham courtroom thriller adaptations *The Client* and *A Time to Kill*, which grossed $92 million and $109 million, respectively. He was tapped by Warner Bros. to take over the *Batman* franchise from Tim Burton, turning out the hugely successful *Batman Forever* (over $330 million worldwide) and the less lucrative *Batman and Robin*. Known for bringing out the best in cast and crew, he's praised by actors for his empathy and self-deprecating humor. But Schumacher, who has described himself as a "pop culture sponge," has taken some knocks from critics. He was eviscerated by some reviewers for his bleak 1999 thriller *8MM*, which, according to *L.A. Times* critic Ken Turan, "made the world a worse place to live." One of the few directors to get his start as a costume designer, Schumacher dreamed up the clothes worn in Woody Allen's *Sleeper* and *Interiors* before turning to screenwriting in the mid-'70s, penning such pics as the 1976 comedy *Car Wash*.

MARTIN SCORSESE

c/o Cappa Productions
445 Park Ave.
Seventh Floor
New York, NY 10022
Phone: (212) 906-8800
Fax: (212) 906-8891
Repped by: Artists Management Group

While indisputably the ultimate "director's director," Scorsese has never presided over a $100 million-plus domestic blockbuster or taken home an Oscar statuette. Still, his stature as a craftsman seems to have lifted him above Hollywood's usual "What have you done for me lately?" attitude. That's due in part to the fact that A-list talent still want to work with the fifty-six-year-old director of *Taxi Driver* and *GoodFellas*. Even the notoriously skittish Leonardo DiCaprio committed to star in the Disney-Warner Bros.' co-prod *Gangs of New York*. A onetime NYU film professor and a supervising editor of the concert documentary *Woodstock*, Scorsese set the tone for his illustrious career with 1973's violent crime drama *Mean Streets*, starring longtime collaborator Robert De Niro. Scorsese's reputation as an artist has managed to get even controversy-averse Hollywood to back such hot-button projects as *The Last Temptation of Christ* and *Kundun*, and from his New York headquarters, Scorsese continues to make the films he wants to.

RIDLEY SCOTT

Scott Free
9348 Civic Center Dr.
Mezzanine Floor
Beverly Hills, CA 90210
Phone: (310) 888-4100
Fax: (310) 888-4111
Repped by:
Creative Artists Agency

The British-born Scott got his start as a set designer for the BBC before becoming a hugely prolific commercial director and forming his own RSA production company in the mid-'60s. His first pic, *The Duelists*, received a measure of critical acclaim, but it wasn't until his first American feature, 1982's *Blade Runner*, that Scott earned himself a place in movie history. While it was no blockbuster commercially, *Blade Runner*'s bleak, post-industrial production design and barely-there lighting would set the visual tone for futuristic thrillers for the next two decades. Scott pushed the envelope again with 1991's controversial, Oscar-nominated drama *Thelma & Louise*, but for the rest of the decade he oversaw a string of misfires including *1492: Conquest of Paradise* (1992), *White Squall* (1996), and *G.I. Jane* (1997). In 1998, Warner Bros. pulled the plug on his bank-breaking Arnold Schwarzenegger–starrer *I Am Legend* during pre-production. Undaunted, Scott quickly segued to DreamWorks' $100 million sandals-and-swords actioner *Gladiator*.

TONY SCOTT

Scott Free

A fine art painter before joining his older brother Ridley's RSA commercial production company in the early '80s, Scott made his feature debut on

TONY SCOTT (CON'T)

9348 Civic Center Dr.
Mezzanine Floor
Beverly Hills, CA 90210
Phone: (310) 888-4100
Fax: (310) 888-4111
Repped by:
Creative Artists Agency

the stylishly sexy vampire thriller *The Hunger* (1983). From there he quickly segued into helming the kind of cynical, formulaic thrill rides—and commercial successes—that the late Don Simpson and Jerry Bruckheimer were famous for, including *Top Gun*, *Beverly Hills Cop II,* and *Days of Thunder*. In 1993, he reclaimed some of his tarnished artistic reputation with the hyper-violent, Quentin Tarantino–scripted artsploitation pic *True Romance*, before getting back on the blockbuster wagon with the Bruckheimer-produced *Crimson Tide* and *Enemy of the State*. The Scott brothers led an investor buyout of London's famed Shepperton Studios in 1995 and masterminded the successful 1997 Showtime series *The Hunger*, based on Tony's early feature. The Scotts moved their base of operations several times during the '90s, jumping from Fox to Disney to the failed PolyGram Films.

TOM SHADYAC

Shady Acres Entertainment
c/o Universal Pictures
100 Universal City Plaza
Bungalow 112
Universal City, CA 91608
Phone: (818) 777-9699
Fax: (818) 866-0175
Repped by:
United Talent Agency

Tom Shadyac's résumé as a director is thin, with only four films, but he's got the goods. With $100 million-plus performers in *Ace Ventura, Pet Detective*; *The Nutty Professor*; *Liar Liar*; and *Patch Adams* under his belt, Shadyac has quickly become a gross player in Hollywood. And through his new deal at Universal, where his films have been studio lifesavers over the last two years, he dictates the terms. Shadyac started his career as the youngest staff joke writer ever (at twenty-three) for Bob Hope. Early films included *Tom, Dick and Harry* and *Franken-*

stein: The College Years. He's one of the "gross out" directors who have made it in recent years, right next to the Farrelly Bros.

RON SHELTON

c/o Shanghai'd Films
2601 Colorado Ave.
Santa Monica, CA 90404
Phone: (310) 453-8337
Fax: (310) 828-3131
Repped by:
Sanford-Gross Agency

Shelton transformed the historically formulaic and macho sports film genre by eschewing the inevitable run-up to the "big game" and instead focusing on complex, anti-heroic men and powerful women. Himself a former minor league infielder and later a sculptor, Shelton entered the Hollywood big leagues in 1983, co-writing and serving as second unit director on the Roger Spottiswoode–helmed political thriller *Under Fire*. He made his feature directing debut on the 1988 Kevin Costner–starrer *Bull Durham*, and followed that a year later with the New Orleans–set political drama *Blaze*. (He later married actress Lolita Davidovich, who portrayed the vivacious title character.) Shelton scored a slam dunk with the basketball pic *White Men Can't Jump* before returning to baseball with *Cobb*, a critically praised but uncommercial profile of the unlikable baseball superstar. He then wrote and directed 1996's golf comedy *Tin Cup*, which delivered sub-par box office results despite the presence of *Durham* star Costner. Shelton is known to rely extensively on rehearsals to help actors clearly define characters and behavior. Hoping to avoid the pitfalls of studio development, in 1998, he teamed up with producer Stephen Chin (*Another Day in Paradise*) to form the indie production outfit Shanghai'd Films. The pair announced plans to make several moderately priced pics per year, some of which Shelton will direct, starting with the prize-fight drama *Play It to the Bone*, starring Antonio Banderas and Woody Harrelson.

STEVEN SODERBERGH

c/o Pat Dollard
Independent Artists Management
7906 Wenwood Blvd.
Suite B
Baton Rouge, LA 70809
Phone: (225) 926-9190
Fax: (225) 924-0149

Steven Soderbergh burst on the indie scene in 1989 with a little piece of anarchy called *sex, lies & videotape*, which thrust him into the limelight as the poster child for the new American indie cinema. Rather than go directly to Studioville, the former game-show scorekeeper went on to make a series of small, idiosyncratic, and generally disregarded films like *King of the Hill*, *Kafka*, *Schizopolis*, and *Gray's Anatomy*. A decade after his debut, Soderbergh, according to many reviewers, realized his potential with Universal's George Clooney/Jennifer Lopez–starrer *Out of Sight*, a sly, sexy caper pic based on Elmore Leonard's playful crime novel. Though the studio bungled its release (putting the smart, adult pic in the crowded, hormonal summer), Soderbergh was back in the critics' (and studios') glowing graces with raves and awards. Soderbergh has served as producer on *Pleasantville* and *The Daytrippers*, and as a director, he recently made *The Limey*; and he's putting finishing touches on the Julia Roberts vehicle *Erin Brockovich*. He doesn't regard his move to studio films (over the indies) as selling out: "America has no shortage of auteurs," he told the *New York Times*. "What we have is a shortage of films being made by smart filmmakers that open in four thousand theaters. I don't understand why a filmmaker should be penalized for working in the mainstream."

BARRY SONNENFELD

Sonnenfeld/Josephson Productions
500 South Buena Vista St.
Animation Building
Suite 3E7
Burbank, CA 91521
Phone: (818) 560-0606
Fax: (818) 556-6662
Repped by:
Creative Artists Agency

Barry Sonnenfeld was a onetime classmate of and cinematographer for the Coen brothers at NYU, not to mention the director of photography on nine porno films, of which he is quite proud. Most of Hollywood, however, has forgotten those salad days with such eye-popping mega-pics as *Wild Wild West*, *Men in Black*, *Get Shorty*, *The Addams Family*, and *Addams Family Values* on his résumé. Ever wry and often incorrigible, Sonnenfeld leans toward comedy, but will explore drama with his upcoming feature on the life of Muhammad Ali with his fave star Will Smith. Under his production pact with Disney, Sonnenfeld has ventured onto the small screen, producing and directing the pilot of *Maximum Bob* for ABC. He and partner Barry Josephson also executive produced the short-lived *Fantasy Island*. Sonnenfeld is without doubt a gross player in Hollywood: When Sony tried to put together the sequel for *Men in Black*, the accumulated gross participation would have totaled 125 percent of the gross. Realizing the ridiculousness of such a scenario, Sonnenfeld bowed out and left such arguments to the rest of the Men in Black (suits).

STEVEN SPIELBERG

c/o DreamWorks SKG

As the most commercially successful director of all time, and arguably the most prosperous producer as well, Spielberg was Hollywood's

STEVEN SPIELBERG (CON'T)

100 Universal City Plaza
Building 477
Universal City, CA 91608
Phone: (818) 733-7000
Fax: (818) 509-1433
Repped by:
Creative Artists Agency

eight-hundred-pound gorilla even before he started his own studio with David Geffen and Jeffrey Katzenberg. One of only a handful of first-dollar gross participants, the fifty-two-year-old director is credited with single-handedly inventing the "event picture" with his 1975 horror pic *Jaws*. Spielberg has continued as the form's chief architect for two and a half decades with such blockbusters as *Raiders of the Lost Ark*, *E.T. The Extra-Terrestrial*, *Hook*, *Jurassic Park*, and *The Lost World*. His talent for cinematic alchemy reached new heights with 1993's *Schindler's List* and 1998's *Saving Private Ryan*, in which Spielberg managed to turn his hellish vision of WWII into box office—and Oscar—gold. As the head of DreamWorks' live-action film activities, Spielberg is notoriously hands-on, phoning in midnight casting decisions and taking pitch meetings. He is entitled to direct three non-DreamWorks films over the next ten years, but the company has typically avoided this by taking a 50 percent co-financing position in any film Spielberg helms for a rival studio, as it did with the Paramount-developed *Ryan* and the Fox-developed Tom Cruise–starrer *Minority Report*.

OLIVER STONE

201 Santa Monica Blvd.
Suite 610
Santa Monica, CA 90401

Oliver Stone manages to piss off just about everyone in Hollywood, whether it's talent, studio chiefs, or other directors. Over the years, he bounced from studio to studio with a handful of production deals for his former Ixtlan Films banner. Though he recently disbanded his Illusion

OLIVER STONE (CON'T)
Phone: (310) 458-7747
Fax: (310) 458-1597
Repped by:
Creative Artists Agency

Entertainment partnership with Dan Halsted to focus on writing and directing rather than producing, he continues to have a place on the A-list and he continues to go for the jugular on whichever controversial subject he chooses: high finance (*Wall Street*), crime (*Natural Born Killers*), assassinations (*JFK*), war (*Platoon*, *Born on the Fourth of July*), or politics (*Nixon*). Though Stone can command a decent deal on films he puts together, it's getting tougher. *U-Turn* was turned down by virtually every studio—despite its lowly $15 million budget guaranteed by Stone—before Stone finagled Phoenix Pictures to come up with the cash. He executive produced the box office no-show *The Corruptor*, but most of 1998 was spent making his NFL football opus for Warner Bros., *Any Given Sunday*.

BETTY THOMAS

Tall Trees
12009-11 Guerin St.
Studio City, CA 91604
Phone: (818) 754-5442
Fax: (818) 754-5443
Repped by:
Creative Artists Agency

Dubbed the "Midnight Queen" for putting her crew members through ridiculously long hours, Betty Thomas has jumped to the rarefied, and mostly male, realm of A-list feature directors with only three feature films to her name, all hits: *The Brady Bunch Movie*, *Private Parts*, and *Dr. Dolittle*. She recently finished production on *28 Days* with Sandra Bullock for Columbia Pictures, and the film is pure Betty Thomas: a serio-comic look at a female gossip journalist sent to rehab. Thomas loves the humor as long as it has a social edge. The tall and gangly Sgt. Lucy Bates on *Hill Street Blues*, Thomas appropriately calls her production company with partner Jenno Topping, Tall Trees Productions. Her impression of comedy in the United States is simple: "If you think it's funny, you're gonna laugh."

PAUL VERHOEVEN

Verhoeven/Marshall
c/o Sony Pictures
10202 West Washington Blvd.
Astaire Building
Culver City, CA 90232
Phone: (310) 244-5352
Fax: (310) 244-2034
Repped by:
Creative Artists Agency

This former documentarian for the Royal Dutch Navy went on to become one of Holland's most successful exports to the film industry and one of Hollywood's more controversial directors. After a series of lauded films back home (*Soldier of Orange*, *The Fourth Man*, and *Flesh + Blood*) Verhoeven received critical and commercial success with his first Hollywood feature, the smirky sci-fi thriller *RoboCop*, which he followed with the sci-fi summer hit *Total Recall* in 1990. But his biggest acclaim to date stems from the campy psycho-thriller *Basic Instinct* in 1992, which garnered plenty of controversy for its graphic sexuality and served as the breakout role for Sharon Stone. While that film courted controversy and became a huge blockbuster, Verhoeven's next film, *Showgirls*, achieved only the former.

Verhoeven then tried to rehab his career by returning to his sci-fi roots, directing the actioner *Starship Troopers*, which failed to live up to its pre-release hype. Verhoeven is hoping for a complete revival with his latest film, *The Hollow Man*, a drama about a man rendered invisible, written by *Air Force One* scribe Andrew Marlowe and starring Kevin Bacon and Elisabeth Shue.

PETER WEIR

c/o Creative Artists Agency
9830 Wilshire Blvd.
Beverly Hills, CA 90212
Phone: (310) 288-4545
Fax: (310) 288-4800

Peter Weir, who began his film career making anti-establishment shorts while he worked for an Australian TV station in the '60s, had one of the best-reviewed films in years with *The Truman Show*, which offered a rare semi-dramatic performance from Jim Carrey. *Truman* was Weir's first film in five years, and re-established the Aussie as one of the global elite filmmakers. Weir was at the forefront of Australia's cinema renaissance of the late '70s, when he helmed such work as *Picnic at Hanging Rock*, *The Last Wave*, *Gallipoli* (which helped launch Mel Gibson's acting career), and *The Year of Living Dangerously*, which landed Weir his first Hollywood film, the thriller *Witness*. The Harrison Ford–starrer earned Weir his first Oscar nomination for Best Director. Ford also starred in Weir's next film, *The Mosquito Coast*, in 1986. Weir's 1989 pic *Dead Poets Society* garnered him a second Oscar nom; and its follow-up, *Green Card*, earned Weir a Best Original Screenplay nomination. Five years before mounting *Truman* (for which he received his third Best Director Oscar nomination), Weir helmed *Fearless*, a drama starring Jeff Bridges, Rosie Perez, and John Turturro. While he hasn't zeroed in on his next outing, Weir has been approached by every studio to helm its highest-profile, star vehicles.

JOHN WOO

Lion Rock Productions

After helming more than twenty-five features in his native Hong Kong, John Woo has experienced the greatest crossover success of any

JOHN WOO (CON'T)

c/o Sony Pictures
10202 West Washington Blvd.
Lean Building
Culver City, CA 90232
Phone: (310) 244-3866
Fax: (310) 244-0668
Repped by:
William Morris Agency

Asian director in Hollywood, whose homegrown directors have been copying his style and technique for years. Woo, who made his Hollywood debut directing Jean-Claude Van Damme in *Hard Target* in 1993, most recently helmed Tom Cruise in the sequel to *Mission: Impossible*. While some have labeled him a one-trick, chopsocky pony, Woo has been widely embraced by Hollywood mavens and many critics alike. Though he has directed such pics as *Killer*, *A Bullet in the Head*, and *Hard-Boiled*, Woo has said his influences come as much from musicals like *West Side Story* and *The Umbrellas of Cherbourg* as from classic American gangster movies. After modest success from *Hard Target*, Woo waited three years before making his first true American studio film, the $55 million John Travolta/Christian Slater vehicle *Broken Arrow*. Woo loves movie stars, and he re-teamed with Travolta for *Face/Off*, which co-starred Nick Cage and went on to earn more than $300 million worldwide. He and partner Terence Chang's Lion Rock Prods. has a first-look production pact with Sony Pictures.

ROBERT ZEMECKIS

c/o ImageMovers
DreamWorks
100 Universal City Plaza
Building 484
Universal City, CA 91608
Phone: (818) 733-8313

In 1997, the forty-five-year-old Oscar-winning director of *Forrest Gump* unwrapped his own box of chocolates, the DreamWorks–based production entity ImageMovers, which he formed with ex-CAA agent Jack Rapke and producing partner Steve Starkey. The company inked a lucrative, five-year deal at DreamWorks, which formalized Zemeckis's twenty-two-year rela-

ROBERT ZEMECKIS (CON'T)

Fax: (818) 733-8333

Repped by: Creative Artists Agency

tionship with co-topper Steven Spielberg. A straight-shooting Midwesterner, "Bob Z," as he's known, has a reputation for clearness of vision and inexhaustible physical stamina. As a helmer, Zemeckis has consistently pushed the limits of film technology—from the ground-breaking animation/live-action hybrid *Who Framed Roger Rabbit* to the time-warp juxtapositions of *Gump*. DreamWorks and Fox recently have teamed up on two features, *What Lies Beneath* and *Cast Away*, from the helmer whose pics have already grossed well over $2 billion worldwide.

MOGULS

BRONFMAN, Edgar, Jr. (Universal Studios) · DILLER, Barry (USA Films and USA Networks) · EISNER, Michael (Walt Disney Company) · GEFFEN, David (DreamWorks/SKG) · IDEI, Nobuyuki (Sony Corporation) · KATZENBERG, Jeffrey (DreamWorks/SKG) · KERKORIAN, Kirk (MGM/UA) · LEVIN, Gerald (Time Warner) · MURDOCH, Rupert (NewsCorporation) · REDSTONE, Sumner (Paramount/Viacom) · TURNER, Ted (Time Warner)

MOGULS

The film business has always had its "moneymen," wealthy entrepreneurs, usually from the East Coast, who are attracted to the glamour of Hollywood.

While it's always been a risky business, moviemaking has in recent years seen shrinking profit margins as the costs of production and marketing have continued to skyrocket while movie attendance has only inched upward. The reliance on foreign and ancillary revenues has further amplified contrast between hits and misses, resulting in wildly uneven and unpredictable revenues.

For that reason, only hugely capitalized, diversified companies can afford to ride out the stomach-churning highs and lows of the business. Today's major studios are all owned by multinational media concerns, several of which are headed by charismatic magnates.

To some extent, of course, these studio owners wield the ultimate power, deciding how much money to pump into moviemaking and firing studio chiefs with the wave of a hand. But in other ways they are at the mercy of a fickle, creative business that doesn't respond to the kind of consolidation and downsizing that have driven much of the financial growth in other sectors for the past few decades.

EDGAR BRONFMAN, JR.
Chairman/CEO
Seagram Co.
c/o Universal Studios
100 Universal City Plaza

In 1995, this part-time songwriter and scion of the Bronfman liquor empire decided to sell Seagram's stake in Du Pont in order to buy MCA (later Universal), a deal that cost the company billions of dollars in lost profits as Du Pont stock soared and MCA foundered. Then in 1998, the younger Bronfman purchased PolyGram from

EDGAR BRONFMAN, JR. (CON'T)

Universal City, CA 91608
Phone: (818) 777-1000
Fax: (818) 866-1440

Dutch electronics giant Phillips for over $10 million, creating the world's largest record empire, and further exposing his family fortune to the vicissitudes of the entertainment business. The plan was to get $1 billion back by selling off PolyGram's film division, although he was able only to sell off certain parts of the company, for considerably less money. Bronfman's other controversial moves have included spinning off a controlling stake in Universal's television production activities to showbiz mogul Barry Diller, and firing former Viacom CEO Frank Biondi—with a $25 million–plus golden parachute. But it was the abysmal performance of the studio's 1997 and 1998 feature slates that caused Bronfman the biggest publicity headaches. Universal suffered through a series of flops including the costly *Babe: A Pig in the City*, *Meet Joe Black*, *Virus*, and *EDtv* before finally turning the tide in the summer of 1999 with *The Mummy*. However, not all of Universal's decisions have met with disapproval from his family—or Wall Street. For instance, GetMusic, Universal Music's Internet joint venture with German media conglom Bertelsmann AG, and the 1999 opening of Universal's second Florida theme park, Islands of Adventure, were both greeted with optimism in financial circles.

BARRY DILLER

Chairman/CEO
USA Films and USA Networks

After his failed bid for Paramount Pictures (the studio he guided to great prosperity from 1974 to 1984) in 1993, Barry Diller avoided the film business for years, before jumping back in with

BARRY DILLER (CON'T)
152 West 52nd St.
42nd Floor
New York, NY 10019
Phone: (212) 314-7300
Fax: (212) 314-7339

both feet in 1999. Without divulging his future plans for the company, Diller formed USA Films (the feature sibling to his USA Networks) with the acquisition of specialized distributor October Films and former PolyGram Filmed Entertainment assets, including Gramercy, Propaganda Films, Interscope Communications, and PolyGram Home Video. Though he appointed former October co-president Scott Greenstein as chairman and former Gramercy prexy Russell Schwartz as president, observers note that it will be Diller's aggressive management style, commercial instincts, and relationships with both Wall Street moneymen and Hollywood creative professionals that will drive USA Films. Industryites wonder whether Diller's ultimate goal is to use USA Films mainly as a content provider for his TV and Internet interests. For now, the banner is going about business in traditional Hollywood style: Its first production will be *One Night at McCools's*, starring Michael Douglas and Liv Tyler; and USA is developing such films as *At Home with the Marquis De Sade* for Gus Van Sant to direct.

MICHAEL EISNER

Chairman/CEO
Walt Disney Company
500 South Buena Vista St.
Team Disney Building
Burbank, CA 91521
Phone: (818) 560-1000

Since joining the company as CEO in 1984, Michael Eisner has guided Disney from a well-known but fading family brand to its current status as a $23-billion-a-year global multimedia juggernaut. The immensely ambitious and hands-on exec oversees the entire spectrum of Disney activities, which includes the live-action and animated motion picture production divisions, theme

MICHAEL EISNER (CON'T)

Fax: (818) 560-1300

parks, the ABC TV network, Disney retail stores, and the company's Internet interests. Not that he works for the fun of it, mind you: Eisner is also one of the world's highest-paid execs, bringing home in 1998 an enormous $589 million in salary, bonus, and exercised stock options. Helping Eisner to revitalize the once moribund Disney were the late president and COO Frank Wells and former Walt Disney Studios chairman Jeffrey Katzenberg, who was fired by Eisner in 1994. Katzenberg subsequently sued his former employer, resulting in a costly, five-year battle and embarrassing revelations about Disney activities. Eisner has publicly tweaked Walt Disney Studios chairman Joe Roth for the company's overspending and lack of moneymakers; and in 1999 he shook up his film corps by expanding the purview of animation chief Peter Schneider to include Walt Disney live-action films—an appointment that led to the exit of production topper David Vogel. Eisner also continues to take flak from critics who feel he should designate a successor and not continue to run the company as a fiefdom.

DAVID GEFFEN

Partner

DreamWorks SKG

100 Universal City Plaza

Building 477

Universal City, CA 91608

The outspoken, openly gay billionaire and co-founder, with Jeffrey Katzenberg and Steven Spielberg, of DreamWorks SKG began his career, like so many others, in the William Morris Agency mailroom in the mid-'60s. In 1969, after brief agenting stints at Ashley Famous and Creative Management, he co-founded a music management company whose clients included singer-song-

DAVID GEFFEN (CON'T)

Phone: (818) 733-7000

Fax: (818) 509-1433

writer Laura Nyro. The following year he founded Asylum Records, eventually becoming chairman of Elektra-Asylum Records, which was later sold to Warner Communications for a reported $7 million. In 1975, when he became vice-chairman of Warner Bros. Pictures, his career was derailed briefly after he was misdiagnosed with cancer. In 1980, he formed Geffen Records as well as the Geffen Film Co., producing such features as *Personal Best* (1982), *Risky Business* (1983), *Lost in America* (1985), *Little Shop of Horrors* (1985), *Beetle Juice* (1988) (exec producer), *Men Don't Leave* (1990), and *Defending Your Life* (1991). In 1990, he sold Geffen Records to MCA, only to turn around and form the David Geffen Company and later DreamWorks.

NOBUYUKI IDEI

President/Co-CEO and Representative Director

Sony Corporation

c/o Sony Corporation of America

550 Madison Ave.

New York, NY 10022-3211

Phone: (212) 833-8000

Tokyo-based Nobuyuki Idei is part of a new breed within the Sony Corporation empire. Aggressive, refined, and well-versed in international marketing dynamics, in 1995 Idei—who had been overseeing corporate communications and advertising as a director and then managing director of the company since 1989—was handed control of Sony Corporation, which includes the Los Angeles movie studio. Since then Sony has embarked on a series of corporate restructurings, including tightening the reins at the movie studio, which under previous management, through overspending and a series of flops, forced Sony to take a $3.2 billion write-off for its film operations. Idei, who eschews much of the traditional Japanese rule-by-committee business model, keeps close tabs on what's happening with Sony Pictures Entertainment chairman John Calley and the top-rung executives in Los Angeles. He has thrown his support behind Calley, though the Tokyo-based exec added another layer of checks and balances when he upped Gotham-based Sony exec Howard Stringer to chairman and CEO of Sony Corporation of America, overseeing both Sony Pictures Entertainment and Sony Music Entertainment, run by Thomas Mottola.

JEFFREY KATZENBERG

Partner

DreamWorks SKG
100 Universal City Plaza
Building 10
Universal City, CA 91608
Phone: (818) 733-7000
Fax: (818) 509-1433

A career studio exec, Katzenberg started out in show business as assistant to Paramount chairman Barry Diller in 1975, rising through the ranks to positions including Par exec director of marketing, VP of programming at Par TV, and VP of feature film production. In 1982, he was made president of production over Par's feature and TV divisions, working closely with Michael Eisner. The pair presided over the studio during the heady '80s with pics including *48 HRS* (1982), *Flashdance* (1983), *Terms of Endearment* (1983), and *Beverly Hills Cop* (1984). In 1984, Katzenberg ankled Par for Disney, following Eisner, who become chairman of Walt Disney Studios. During his ten-year run he, Eisner, and Disney president and CEO Frank Wells oversaw the rebuilding of Disney's feature animation division with *The Little Mermaid* (1989), *Beauty and the Beast* (1991), and *Aladdin* (1992). In 1994, *The Lion King* became the highest-grossing animated pic ever. But when he was passed over for corporate no. 2 post after Wells died, Katzenberg resigned. Later that same year, he, Steven Spielberg, and David Geffen announced the formation of DreamWorks SKG, where Katzenberg's day-to-day focus is on animation. While his long-term goal is clearly to beat his old company at their game, DreamWorks had good but not great results with its first two animated outings, *The Prince of Egypt* and *Antz*, a co-production with digital animation house PDI.

KIRK KERKORIAN

Director/President and CEO

Tracinda Corporation
c/o Metro-Goldwyn-Mayer
2500 Broadway
Santa Monica, CA 90404-3061
Phone: (310) 449-3000

This former commercial pilot, airline magnate, and Vegas hotelier has the distinction of buying the same studio, MGM, three times in three decades. After first purchasing the studio in 1970 and becoming its CEO in 1974, he spearheaded MGM's takeover of United Artists in the late '70s to form MGM/UA. But in 1985 he sold MGM to Turner Broadcasting, only to turn around and buy back UA and the MGM production and distribution companies, while Turner retained the MGM library. Five years later he sold MGM to French studio Pathe, which defaulted on its loan. In 1996, Kerkorian backed a management-led buyout of the ailing studio from the French bank Credit Lyonnaise. As the studio continued to founder financially, turning out flop after flop, Kerkorian was forced to pump cash into it. In 1999, longtime studio topper Frank Mancuso stepped down and was replaced by Alex Yemenidjian, longtime Kerkorian aide and the CEO of his MGM Grand casino company.

GERALD LEVIN

Chairman/CEO
Time Warner
75 Rockefeller Plaza
New York, NY 10019
Phone: (212) 484-8000
Fax: (212) 956-2847

This former civil rights and First Amendment attorney has worked for Time Inc. since 1972, when he joined the company's fledgling cable enterprise, Home Box Office, as vice-president of programming. He gradually moved up (and sometimes down) the corporate ladder until eventually ascending to chairman of Time Warner in 1992. Known as a low-key, innovative, and often visionary figure, Levin has driven Time Warner's vast media empire into its current position as a global leader. Although he has fumbled some of his dealmaking opportunities, including the 1980 failure to acquire Columbia Pictures, his career is marked by more successful endeavors, most notably helping to engineer the monumental 1989 merger of Time Inc. and Warner Communications. And in 1996, Levin oversaw the $1 billion merger of Time Warner and Turner Entertainment (whose holdings included TBS, CNN, and New Line Cinema). Though just a few years ago Time Warner stock was stagnating and many were calling for his head, today Levin's empire is a Wall Street darling. The company's strength is spread throughout, with strong contributions from each division, including Warner Bros. Studios, which has seen a turnaround thanks to such recent hits as *The Matrix* and *Analyze This*.

RUPERT MURDOCH

Chairman/CEO

The Aussie mogul has come a long way from his newspaper roots, building a truly global media conglomerate with its hands in film (Fox Filmed

RUPERT MURDOCH (CON'T)
NewsCorporation
c/o 20th Century Fox
10201 West Pico Blvd.
Building 100
Los Angeles, CA 90035
Phone: (310) 369-1000
Fax: (310) 369-3846

Entertainment, which includes 20th Century Fox, Fox 2000, Fox Searchlight, and Fox Animation Studios), TV (Fox Sports Net and the Fox TV network), newspapers (*New York Post*, *London Times*), publishing (HarperCollins), satellite systems (BskyB), and sports (L.A. Dodgers), among others. Though his focus is on the global pie, and not necessarily on his film operations, with a string of record-breaking and bank-filling worldwide hits like *Titanic*, *There's Something About Mary*, *The Full Monty*, and *Independence Day*, Murdoch has to be happy with his powerhouse film studio/distribution company. However, that success puts added pressure on Fox to continue its moneymaking days, leaving little room for creative risk, as Murdoch continues his acquisitive ways, looking for new entities to add to his growing empire. Though a risk-taker, Murdoch resolutely avoids hands-on management of his subsidiaries, leaving the day-to-day decisions to such execs as NewsCorp. prexy and COO Peter Chernin and Fox Filmed Entertainment topper Bill Mechanic.

SUMNER REDSTONE

Chairman of the Board/CEO
Viacom
1515 Broadway
52nd Floor
New York, NY 10036
Phone: (212) 258-6000

Redstone is the only one of the current crop of media moguls who started his showbiz career as a theater owner, and the tight-fisted approach he developed in the low-margin world of exhibition still colors the operations at Paramount. A first lieutenant in the U.S. Army during WWII, Redstone graduated from Harvard Law School in 1947 and worked as a lawyer in various public and private capacities until the mid-'50s. He then became executive VP of the Northeast

Drive-In Theater Corp., and in 1967, president and CEO of Massachusetts-based circuit National Amusements, which owns over 80 percent of Viacom. He later became chairman of Viacom, a TV producer/syndicator and parent company of cable nets MTV, Nickelodeon, and Showtime. Redstone famously survived a Boston hotel fire in 1979, losing the use of one hand. But the costliest battle of his life started in 1993, with Barry Diller over the purchase of Paramount Communications. Redstone eventually bought Par for $10 billion—$2 billion more than he originally offered—as well as vidstore chain giant Blockbuster Entertainment. He installed Sherry Lansing and Jonathan Dolgen as heads of Par and has at least partially realized his long-held goal of corporate synergy with the success of MTV Films.

TED TURNER

Vice-Chairman
Time Warner
75 Rockefeller Plaza
New York, NY 10019
Phone: (212) 484-8000
Fax: (212) 956-2847

When Ted Turner sold his flourishing Turner Entertainment to Time Warner in 1996, everyone assumed that it was all part of his master plan to take over Time Warner. Now, nearly four years later, the brash entertainment mogul has not moved a muscle in that direction. He's currently the largest single holder of Time Warner stock, allowing him, by his own estimation, to quietly keep tabs on things at Time Warner. Turner is clearly pleased by the performance of New Line Cinema, which was one of his contributions to the TW empire. He made headlines in 1997 when he donated $1 billion to benefit United Nations agencies.

PERCENTERS

(Agents and Managers)

ADDIS, Keith, and Nick Wechsler (Industry Entertainment) · BERG, Jeffrey S. (ICM) · BERKUS, Jim (UTA) · BOOKMAN, Robert (CAA) · BURNHAM, John, and Mike Simpson (WMA) · ELWES, Cassian (WMA) · ENDEAVOR Agency · GREY, Brad (Brillstein-Grey Entertainment) · HOWARD, Toni (ICM) · HUVANE, Kevin (CAA) · KAMINS, Ken (ICM) · LIMATO, Ed (ICM) · LOURD, Bryan (CAA) · LOVETT, Richard (CAA) · NEWMAN, Robert (ICM) · NICITA, Rick (CAA) · O'CONNOR, David (CAA) · OVITZ, Michael (AMG) · PTAK, John (CAA) · QUEALLY, Hylda (WMA) · RIFKIN, Arnold (WMA) · SANFORD, Geoffrey (The Sanford-Gross Agency) · SCOTT, Joan (Writers & Artists Agency) · STEVENS, Nick, and John Lesher (UTA) · 3 ARTS ENTERTAINMENT (Erwin Stoff, Howard Klein, and Michael Rotenberg) · WIATT, Jim (WMA) · WIRTSCHAFTER, Dave (ICM) · YORN, Rick, and Julie Silverman Yorn (AMG)

PERCENTERS

(Agents and Managers)

No longer viewed as leisure-suited reptiles forced to enter through studios' back gates, agents and personal managers today hold a shaky but impressive grasp on the power strings of Hollywood—and, for that matter, popular culture in general. Most credit former MCA topper Lew Wasserman, and later CAA co-founder Michael Ovitz, with transforming the percenters' image from flesh-peddling carnival barkers to stately, knowledgeable businessmen who control the talent and material the studios need. Their status was so elevated in the late '80s and early '90s that even Wall Street mavens would come calling, looking for guidance in navigating the Byzantine rituals of Hollywood dealmaking.

But don't be fooled by the slick, confident faces worn by these highly paid reps; they cover the reality that agents and managers are the most beleaguered of Hollywood players, always under fire from competitors and insecure in the knowledge that their clout rests exclusively with their clients, those needy, fickle creative types. Moreover, in the last couple of years, changes in the entertainment landscape have put the traditionally hospitable and collaborative working relationships between agents and managers on the precipice of an all-out holy war. Managers are not governed by the same laws and guild restrictions that govern agents (which include being barred from producing their clients' TV shows and features, and legally prevented from charging more than a 10 percent commission). Many agents affect the moral high ground that the lack of regulation of managers is not always in the best interest of the clients, and that managers' freedom to produce their clients' projects is a conflict of interest. Agents would really like the state of California and the talent guilds either to regulate managers in the same way as agents, or deregulate agents so that they have the same liberties as managers.

The growing tension was brought to the forefront in the past few years with the high-profile lawsuit brought by Garry Shandling against his former manager Brad Grey, as well as Creative Artists Agency's refusal to share clients with their former leader Michael Ovitz's new management-production firm, Artists Management Group, which the CAA brass claimed, after losing actor Robin Williams and his agent Mike Menchel to AMG, was actively poaching the agency's clients and agents.

While the relationships between the agents and managers will continue to mutate, either for better or for worse, there is no doubt that both sides will maintain an enormous role in the Hollywood power structure.

The following includes reps, who are either owners, partners, or heads of departments in small and large agencies, as well as the heads of the premier management/production shingles. They all have one thing in common: They handle the careers of the town's hottest writers, directors, actors, and producers.

KEITH ADDIS AND NICK WECHSLER

Industry Entertainment
955 South Carrillo Dr.
Suite 300
Los Angeles, CA 90048
Phone: (323) 954-9000
Fax: (323) 954-9009

In mid-1998 Industry Entertainment partners Keith Addis and Nick Wechsler were enjoying the fruits of their enviable success—a billowing bank account following the 1997 sale of a majority stake to the Interpublic Group of Companies and a client list that included several of the hottest actors in Hollywood. What a difference a few months can make! By the beginning of 1999, the company was nearly decimated by the defections of top managers Rick Yorn and sister-in-law Julie Silverman Yorn, who left to join Michael Ovitz at Artists Management Group, taking their clients (who include Leonardo DiCaprio, Claire Danes, Cameron Diaz, Samuel L. Jackson, and Minnie Driver) and several managers with them. While Industry still represents Jeff Goldblum, Richard Dreyfuss, Angelina Jolie, Billy Bob Thornton, and Ted Danson, among others, much of the company's strength now comes from its production side (overseen by Wechsler), which, according to the brass, initiates three-quarters of its production projects independent of its management clientele. Industry gets in on the ground floor of most of its films, optioning material and often funding development with its production deal and discretionary fund set up at New Line Cinema. Among the films Industry is producing are *Quills*, starring Kate Winslet and Geoffrey Rush, for Fox Searchlight, and *Fifteen Minutes*, starring Robert DeNiro and Edward Burns, for New Line.

JEFFREY S. BERG

Chairman/CEO

International Creative Management

8942 Wilshire Blvd.

Beverly Hills, CA 90211

Phone: (310) 550-4000

Fax: (310) 550-4100

Berg is widely regarded by colleagues and competitors alike as one of the smartest, most adept dealmakers in the business. Under his tutelage ICM became and remains one of the industry's Big Three (along with CAA and William Morris) full-service literary and talent agencies—an international powerhouse (with offices in Los Angeles, New York, London, and Dublin) that offers a hearty blend of A-list talent, cutting-edge directors, acclaimed literary figures, and well-connected producers. Once mocked for preaching the gospel of internationalism, Berg—who has been the driving force behind some of the landmark deals in Hollywood history, including structuring George Lucas's pact with 20th Century Fox for *Star Wars*, a deal that continues to pay ICM big dividends—now is getting some long-awaited vindication as Hollywood thinks and acts globally. In recent years, Berg has turned his attention away from much of the day-to-day hand-holding of the agency business, but he continues to assist agents in navigating intricate deals, help sign new clients, and personally handle such high-profile clients as Francis Ford Coppola, James L. Brooks, Bernardo Bertolucci, Dustin Hoffman, and Barbra Streisand.

His chilly exterior has been his Achilles' heel, but as one colleague put it, "How many agents can you point to who have actually elevated their profession? Jeff has."

JIM BERKUS

Chairman
United Talent Agency
9560 Wilshire Blvd.
Suite 500
Beverly Hills, CA 90212
Phone: (310) 273-6700
Fax: (310) 247-1111

The UCLA law school grad is the top exec at the talent-literary agency that for most of its eight years has been synonymous with turmoil. Formed in 1991 by the merger of Bauer-Benedek and Leading Artists agencies, UTA has surprised all watchers (who predicted its imminent implosion in the mid-'90s) by weathering the storms that upended much of the progress it had gained in the industry. Now matured and stabilized, under Berkus's leadership UTA has become the home of cutting-edge comic talent and emerging, hip writers and directors. On its roster are Jim Carrey, Ben Stiller, Vince Vaughn, Janeane Garofalo, and Martin Lawrence; and directors Tom Shadyac (*Liar Liar*), Wes Anderson (*Rushmore*), the Coen brothers (*Fargo*), David O. Russell (*Spanking the Monkey*), and Paul Thomas Anderson (*Boogie Nights*). Berkus's power was solidified when co-chairman Marty Bauer exited in 1997, and Berkus assumed sole chairmanship. In addition to the day-to-day administrative oversight of the more than

50 agents, Berkus handles such clients as Anderson, Lawrence, the Coen bros., Curtis Hanson (*L.A. Confidential*) and Ron Underwood (*City Slickers*).

ROBERT BOOKMAN

Literary Agent

Creative Artists Agency
9830 Wilshire Blvd.
Beverly Hills, CA 90212
Phone: (310) 288-4545
Fax: (310) 288-4800

A gentleman and a scholar in a business largely populated by barbarians, Bookman is one of the industry's most erudite and connected agents. He serves as CAA's link to the literary worlds both in New York and overseas. And unlike many of his younger colleagues, who grew up in the shadow of Michael Ovitz, Bookman enjoys the press and understands the power of media in advancing his clients' careers. While he made his mark brokering some of the biggest book-to-film deals in history (including the $3 million deal with Fox 2000 for Richard Preston's *Cobra Event*), he adds to his clout by representing such A-list writers and directors as Michael Crichton, Harold Gould, Cameron Crowe, William Goldman, and Olivia Goldsmith. Afraid of losing one of the most respected literary agents in Hollywood, CAA struck a deal with Bookman by which the Francofile now has a management role in the company.

JOHN BURNHAM AND MIKE SIMPSON

Co-Heads

Motion Picture Department

One of the longest-running management teams in Hollywood, Burnham and Simpson have pretty much overseen the day-to-day of WMA's film department since 1989, when they were appointed co-heads of the West Coast

JOHN BURNHAM AND MIKE SIMPSON (CON'T)
William Morris Agency
151 El Camino Dr.
Beverly Hills, CA 90212
Phone: (310) 859-4000
Fax: (310) 859-4462

motion picture arm, reporting to a fiery but largely absent Sue Mengers. Though Jim Wiatt is the top film executive at the percentery, his duties as prexy of WMA put Burnham and Simpson in the driver's seat for the agency's film endeavors.

Simpson, a tall, soft-spoken Texan, is highly regarded internally and outside the agency for his acumen with numbers and his straightforwardness. Though he has been knocked for his lack of "schmoozability," he has managed to attract and keep such clients as directors Tim Burton, Alfonso Arau, Kevin Reynolds, John Woo, and Quentin Tarantino. If Simpson is Mr. Inside, Burnham is Mr. Outside, the more gregarious and party-loving of the two. Known for his wit, mercurial charm, and a tenacity that makes him incapable of accepting the word no, Burnham is criticized for the same traits for which he is praised. The Beverly Hills native represents such actors as Diane Keaton, John Cusack, and Woody Allen, and filmmakers Gus Van Sant, Buck Henry, Philip Kaufman, and Stephen Frears.

Though they're two of the agency's more senior execs, Burnham and Simpson have a hard time motivating their troops, who are often flustered by their lack of management skills.

CASSIAN ELWES

Head of WMA Independent
William Morris Agency

Since joining William Morris in 1994 as vice-president of the percentery's new independent film department (following a lukewarm career as a producer of such pics as *The Chase* and *Men at*

CASSIAN ELWES (CON'T)

151 El Camino Dr.
Beverly Hills, CA 90212
Phone: (310) 859-4000
Fax: (310) 859-4462

Work), Elwes has created a vital player in the worldwide indie marketplace. WMA Independent focuses on packaging indie films and repping them for domestic and international distribution. Among the distribution deals Elwes has negotiated are Robert Duvall's *The Apostle*, which he sold to October Films during the 1997 Toronto Film Festival for more than $5 million, and the still-disputed sale to Miramax of Mark Illsley's 1999 Sundance pic *Happy, Texas*, for what the buyer claimed was $2.5 million but what Elwes has told insiders was closer to $11 million. While many question the economic viability of indie films, compared with packaging TV shows or A-list studio projects, since studios are cutting back on the number of films they make, insiders say Elwes provides an internal service that keeps clients employed and keeps business in-house rather than losing it to a rival. WMA Independent allows clients such as Bruce Willis and John Travolta the opportunity to make pet projects, and in some cases the clients actually own the films' copyrights (like Willis and *Breakfast of Champions*).

ENDEAVOR AGENCY

9701 Wilshire Blvd.
Beverly Hills, CA 90212
Phone: (310) 248-2000
Fax: (310) 248-2020

A relative upstart in the agency business, Endeavor was founded ignominiously in 1995 when Ariel Emanuel, Tom Strickler, David Greenblatt, and Rick Rosen left ICM in the middle of the night to become owner/operators of their own literary and talent agency. They were later joined as partners by Marty Adelstein, David Lonner, Adam Venit, and Doug Robinson from CAA; Steve Rabineau from ICM; and manager-cum-agent Brian Swardstrom. Since then, Endeavor has been on an aggressive growth curve, and with its firm footing in the TV world (through clients such as *Ally McBeal* and *The Practice* creator David E. Kelley). With that foundation, Endeavor has become an alternative to the other, larger major agencies, namely CAA, ICM, and William Morris.

Among its film clients are writers Shane Black (*Lethal Weapon*), Aaron Sorkin (*A Few Good Men*), and Scott Alexander and Larry Karaszewski (*The People vs. Larry Flynt*); and directors Phillip Noyce (*Patriot Games*), David Lynch (*Blue Velvet*), Jon Turteltaub (*Phenomenon*) and Brad Silberling (*City of Angels*). Though the agency has been criticized for not having any A-list names on the talent side, Endeavor's growing actors' list includes Adam Sandler, Edward Norton, Minnie Driver, Jeff Goldblum, Bill Paxton, David Spade, and Lisa Kudrow.

BRAD GREY

Chairman

Brillstein-Grey Entertainment

9150 Wilshire Blvd.

Suite 350

Beverly Hills, CA 90212

Phone: (310) 275-6135

Fax: (310) 275-6180

Since late 1995, when industry legend Bernie Brillstein ceded the day-to-day control of Brillstein-Grey Entertainment to his younger colleague, Brad Grey, the company has continued to flourish, setting a quasi-standard for Hollywood management-production companies. Grey subsequently bought out Brillstein's stake in the company, although Brillstein continues to have an active role in BG. The firm's strength has come primarily from producing such TV series as *NewsRadio*, *Just Shoot Me,* and *The Garry Shandling Show*, and on the management side, handling A-listers Brad Pitt, Nicolas Cage, Sylvester Stallone, Courtney Cox, and Adam Sandler. Grey recently inked a deal with Columbia TriStar TV and a feature deal with Miramax Films. Though TV has defined the company to date, Brillstein-Grey has increased its film activity, producing such pics as *The Replacement Killers* and the upcoming films *Charlie and the Chocolate Factory* for Warner Bros. and *What Planet Are You From?*, with Mike Nichols helming, for Columbia Pictures. On the downside, Grey has had to contend with a high-profile lawsuit brought by former client Garry Shandling, who contends that Grey used his position to make TV deals that benefited him and not Shandling; and that as Grey's cornerstone client, he is responsible for the success of BG's TV production company and entitled to a share of the profits. Observers note that the case could have wide-ranging effects on Hollwood's service sector as it addresses the inherent issue of manager-producer conflict of interest.

TONI HOWARD

Head of Motion Picture Talent

International Creative Management
8942 Wilshire Blvd.
Beverly Hills, CA 90211

Toni Howard, a former casting agent, has been with ICM since 1990, when she moved from the William Morris Agency. Tough and volatile, Howard runs the day-to-day operations of ICM's talent department. Among the clients she personally handles are Cher, James Spader, Samuel L. Jackson, Albert Brooks, and Anjelica Huston. Howard is just one of several top female agents

TONI HOWARD (CON'T)

Phone: (310) 550-4000

Fax: (310) 550-4100

who maintain ICM's hold on some of the biggest names in the business. Working with Howard is Gotham-based senior VP Elaine Goldsmith-Thomas, another tough cookie whose name on a call sheet can make the most hardened studio exec cower. Goldsmith-Thomas represents Julia Roberts, Spike Lee, and Tim Robbins, making her arguably one of the most powerful agents in the biz. ICM's Gotham office is also home to agent Aleen Keshishian, who has helped nurture numerous young actors into stars, including Natalie Portman and Skeet Ulrich.

KEVIN HUVANE

Agent and Managing Director

Creative Artists Agency

9830 Wilshire Blvd.

Beverly Hills, CA 90212

Phone: (310) 288-4545

Fax: (310) 288-4800

Huvane is one of the now well-known Young Turks who was groomed at Michael Ovitz's knee and later pushed for more of a stake in CAA. He and longtime colleague Bryan Lourd have been called the Murderers' Row of talent reps. Armed with a shorthand developed since their days in the William Morris mailroom, along with ample charm and drive, when they focus on an actor, they are nearly impossible to refuse. Huvane grew up in New York and served as an assistant in Morris' Gotham office after Fordham University. Huvane, Lourd (with whom he joined CAA in 1988), and ICM's Ed Limato, are regarded as the best actors' agents in the business. Colleagues and competitors say that Huvane's Irish temper can be devastating if you're on the other end; and he often plays the tough cop for the agency. Huvane represents such talent as Brad Pitt, Sandra Bullock, Keanu Reeves, Nicole Kidman, Janet Jackson, and Meryl Streep.

KEN KAMINS

Senior Vice President/ Head of Motion Picture Literary Department and International Operations Division

International Creative Management
8942 Wilshire Blvd.
Beverly Hills, CA 90211
Phone: (310) 550-4000
Fax: (310) 550-4100

Ken Kamins is regarded as one of the "good guys" in a field where nice guys routinely finish last. Since joining ICM nearly eight years ago, Kamins has made a pastime out of collecting job titles, rising to pulling double duty as head of the agency's literary department as well as head of international operations. He splits these managerial duties with the day-to-day hand-holding of such clients as directors John Frankenheimer, Alan Rudolph, Sidney Lumet, John Boorman, and Robert Altman—a client list that has led his office to be dubbed "the cryogenics lab." As leader of ICM's international operations division, Kamins works in conjunction with Gotham-based agent Bart Walker and ICM's U.K. chairman Duncan Heath and London agent Lyndsey Posner to expand the percentery's role in the independent financing of film and TV projects on behalf of ICM clients, as well as to increase co-production activity in Europe. During his tenure, Kamins has had a hand in putting together numerous international co-productions involving ICM clients, including a complicated deal with New Line Cinema to set up Peter Jackson's *Lord of the Rings* trilogy.

ED LIMATO

Co-President and Vice Chairman

International Creative Management
8942 Wilshire Blvd.

Limato's annual pre–Academy Awards party (which draws more celebs and power figures than almost any Oscar fete) alone puts him near the top of most industryites' power lists, but it's his formidable, loyal client list that makes him one of the most influential players in the film game today. Among his devoted clients are Mel

ED LIMATO (CON'T)
Beverly Hills, CA 90211
Phone: (310) 550-4000
Fax: (310) 550-4100

Gibson, Michelle Pfeiffer, Denzel Washington, Winona Ryder, and Richard Gere—many of whom he has represented since they were cutting their teeth in supporting roles in B movies.

Though his sartorial and social tastes verge on the flamboyant (he has been known to tromp barefoot in the office, sleep in meetings, and finish a browbeating of an unprepared visitor with a Oscar Wilde–like "And by the way, I'm Ed Limato"), Limato bears little resemblance to agenting's flesh-peddling "Sweet Smell of Success"–era predecessors. Colleagues point out that among his strengths as an agent, Limato has an unparalleled sense of Hollywood history that he tries to translate into the larger scope of his clients' careers, helping them build a body of work that hopefully will have resonance and longevity.

BRYAN LOURD

Agent and Managing Director
Creative Artists Agency
9830 Wilshire Blvd.
Beverly Hills, CA 90212
Phone: (310) 288-4545
Fax: (310) 288-4800

Lourd grew up in New Iberia, La., before taking a spin through Cambridge University, George Washington University, and the University of Southern California. After a stint working as a page at CBS, he landed at William Morris in 1983. Like Huvane, he came to CAA from Morris in 1988, and they continue to work in tandem and share clients, including Demi Moore, Keanu Reeves, Brad Pitt, Nicole Kidman, and Ralph Fiennes. Lourd also guides the careers of Madonna, George Clooney, Kristen Scott Thomas, Matthew McConaughey, and Ethan Hawke.

Lourd, who was briefly married to Carrie

Fisher, is highly regarded for his straightforwardness and charm. Studio execs say they trust him and are willing to work with him to far greater extents than many of his colleagues inside and outside CAA. While he and Richard Lovett are viewed as the leaders of the agency, several industry insiders note that they wouldn't be surprised to see Lourd at the head of a studio one day.

RICHARD LOVETT

President
Creative Artists Agency
9830 Wilshire Blvd.
Beverly Hills, CA 90212
Phone: (310) 288-4545
Fax: (310) 288-4800

The seemingly unassuming Wisconsin native is credited with keeping the percentery together following the departure of Michael Ovitz and former president Ron Meyer (to Universal) in 1995. Aggressively ambitious, Lovett began running staff meetings just a few days after Ovitz announced that he was decamping for Disney—and he hasn't looked back since. The Young Turk's leadership abilities and fortitude once earned him the nickname "L'Ovitz," a moniker that has long been buried, particularly after Lovett and CAA declared war on Ovitz's new management firm, Artists Management Group, which was accused of poaching CAA clients and agents. Lovett, whose motivational tactics include E-mailing "thoughts of the day" to his staffers, lives and breathes CAA, which is one reason the former house of Ovitz is still regarded as the top-notch shop when it comes to the representation of marquee names. In addition to overseeing the agency's course, Lovett looks after Tom Hanks, Steven Spielberg, Nicolas Cage, Hugh Grant, and Ron Howard. He has been at CAA since 1983, starting as an assistant to Fred Specktor, the veteran agent who helped guide the careers of Robert De Niro and Danny DeVito.

ROBERT NEWMAN

Senior Vice President and Literary Agent
International Creative Management
8942 Wilshire Blvd.
Beverly Hills, CA 90211
Phone: (310) 550-4000
Fax: (310) 550-4100

Since the departure of CAA's Jack Rapke from the agenting business, Robert Newman has emerged as the most influential and respected directors' agent in the industry. Credited with impeccable taste and unwavering resolve, Newman doesn't target other agency's lists to build his own; rather, he trusts his own prescient eye for talent, which he has used to pluck from obscurity and launch to the mainstream such directors as Robert Rodriguez (*El Mariachi*), Danny Boyle (*Trainspotting*), Edward Burns (*Brothers McMullen*), Baz Luhrmann (*William Shakespeare's Romeo + Juliet*), Guy Ritchie (*Lock, Stock and Two Smoking Barrels*), Peter Cattaneo (*The Full Monty*), Atom Egoyan (*The Sweet Hereafter*), Alex Proyas (*Dark City*), Steven Norrington (*Blade*), and Darren Aronofsky (*Pi*).

The former Miramax distribution exec also handles directors Wes Craven *(Scream),* Gary Fleder (*Kiss the Girls*), Luc Besson (*The Fifth Element*), and Mike Figgis (*Leaving Las Vegas*). It's not uncommon to hear rival agents declaring that they want to build a "Newman business" or that they are seeking to establish a presence in the indie world "like Newman."

RICK NICITA

Co-Chairman

Creative Artists Agency
9830 Wilshire Blvd.
Beverly Hills, CA 90212
Phone: (310) 288-4545
Fax: (310) 288-4800

Since Ron Meyer left CAA to become president and chief operating officer at MCA, Nicita, another convert from William Morris, has served as a key player in unifying the agency in the post-Ovitz era. He's viewed as an affable bridge between the older generation of agents at CAA and the Young Turks (Richard Lovett, Kevin Huvane, Bryan Lourd, and David O'Connor), who assumed leadership roles in late 1995. Nicita also wins kudos from his peers for his soft-spoken style, which conceals a dogged dedication to his job. He is married to Paula Wagner, a former actress, who left her position as an agent at CAA to go into business with Nicita's client Tom Cruise in a production company based at Paramount. Nicita joined CAA in 1980 after twelve years at William Morris. The Wesleyan University grad began his career in Morris's New York mailroom in 1968, before moving to the percentery's Beverly Hills office eight years later. Among those Nicita reps, in addition to Cruise, are Anthony Hopkins, Kenneth Branagh, Marlon Brando, Jeff Bridges, Kevin Kline, and Al Pacino.

DAVID O'CONNOR

Agent and Managing Partner

Creative Artists Agency
9830 Wilshire Blvd.
Beverly Hills, CA 90212
Phone: (310) 288-4545
Fax: (310) 288-4800

O'Connor, who is called "Doc" by his friends, began his career at CAA in 1983, after a three-year stint working as a producer for New Jersey Public Television (WNET). The Dartmouth grad is considered the most affable and grounded of the Young Turks, and he flourishes as one of the agency's behind-the-scenes leaders. O'Connor represents an array of actors, directors, producers, and writers that includes Robert Redford, Sean Connery, Warren Beatty, Chris Columbus, Ted Demme, Sydney Pollack, Jerry Bruckheimer, and Paul Attanasio.

MICHAEL OVITZ

Manager and Co-Founder
Artists Management Group
9465 Wilshire Blvd.
Suite 519
Beverly Hills, CA 90212
Phone: (310) 860-8000
Fax: (310) 271-9753

"He's baaaaack" was the cry heard 'round Hollywood in late 1998 when the man once touted as the most powerful agent in Hollywood returned to the ranks of talent representatives. In January 1999, Ovitz and in-laws Rick Yorn and Julie Silverman Yorn opened their management-production banner, Artists Management Group; and almost immediately Ovitz was accused of stealing executives, poaching clients, and all but destroying an entire company (management-production firm Industry Entertainment, where the Yorns had served as co-presidents).

Moreover, less than two months after opening AMG's doors, the Sun Tsu disciple's former protégés at Creative Artists Agency declared war on AMG. At the time, CAA, stung by the defections of client Robin Williams and agent Mike Menchel to AMG, offered an ultimatum: Clients repped by both companies would have to choose between the agency and the management firm. Since then Ovitz has managed to bring some of his fomer clients into the AMG fold, including directors Barry Levinson and Martin Scorsese.

With its base of hot young talent (including Leonardo DiCaprio and Cameron Diaz) AMG looks to be the most successful endeavor Ovitz has taken on since leaving CAA in 1995.

Though he might have wanted to conquer the world in a different way, as those who worked with him have said, one of Ovitz's favorite expressions was "The past is prologue." Now as a manager, Ovitz has not only the access to stars but also the freedom to package and produce their films.

JOHN PTAK

Head of International Department
Creative Artists Agency
9830 Wilshire Blvd.
Beverly Hills, CA 90212
Phone: (310) 288-4545
Fax: (310) 288-4800

John Ptak, together with Emanuel Nunez, is responsible for packaging, arranging financing, and handling distribution deals for independent films at Creative Artists Agency. A former William Morris agent, he arguably blazed the trail for agency representation of indie films at the beginning of the '90s by arranging financing and setting up such client pics as *Green Card* and *Dances with Wolves*. Ptak also has developed a strategy of repping production companies, such as Ridley and Tony Scott's Scott Free Prods., Sydney Pollack's Mirage Enterprises, and Jean Doumanian's Sweetland Films (which produces all of Woody Allen's films). CAA regularly helps these companies finance their independent pictures by negotiating the domestic and/or foreign distribution arrangements (examples include *Sliding Doors* and *Dancing at Lughnasa*). But unlike many of their counterparts at other agencies, Ptak and Nunez remain active as traditional agents, with day-to-day clients who include Ridley and Tony Scott, Vincent Ward, Peter Weir, and Antonio Banderas.

HYLDA QUEALLY

Senior Vice-President and Head of North American Motion Picture Talent

William Morris Agency
151 El Camino Dr.
Beverly Hills, CA 90212
Phone: (310) 859-4000
Fax: (310) 859-4462

Queally, who was upped in early 1999 to head of North American motion picture talent for William Morris, filled a job that previously had been held by two men (Michael Gruber and Brian Gersh, who both left the agency). The promotion served to stabilize the agency after several recent exits. In addition to overseeing the talent departments in both Hollywood and New York, Queally continues to represent a stalwart list of actors that includes Kate Winslet, Cate Blanchett, Robin Wright Penn, Joseph Fiennes, William Hurt, Frances McDormand, John Malkovich, Nigel Hawthorne, Miranda Richardson, Rufus Sewell, and Eddie Izzard. One of the few female agents to run an agency department, Queally has taken a relatively unorthodox path to get there. She joined the Triad agency in 1989 directly from Dublin, where she ran her own talent agency, representing a large number of Ireland's actors. Born in County Clare, on the southwest coast of Ireland, Queally cut short a career in the London financial world to return home in the mid-'80s to start her talent agency, of which there were few.

ARNOLD RIFKIN

Former President and Worldwide Head of Motion Pictures

William Morris Agency

In July 1999, Rifkin was handed the shocking news that he was being replaced by former ICM co-chairman Jim Wiatt. Rifkin, who was reportedly caught off guard by the change, said at the time that he did not have concrete plans for the future, but he is expected to work as a manager with several clients of long-standing, including Bruce Willis, Whoopi Goldberg, and Danny Glover. Though Rifkin had been the top film

ARNOLD RIFKIN (CON'T)

151 El Camino Dr.
Beverly Hills, CA 90212
Phone: (310) 859-4000
Fax: (310) 859-4462

presence in William Morris management, he had to spend the last few years making up for ground lost with his staffers who felt betrayed by his flirtation with the top production post at Sony Pictures in 1996. Since then Rifkin—who recommitted to the agency in that same year, inking a long-term contract and later accepting the promotion to president—seemed to drift behind the scenes, taking less of a role as the agency's talent-signing frontman. According to staffers, who admit that the emigre from New York's furrier industry felt burned by the press coverage of his attempted, clandestine talks with Sony, Rifkin spent his time revamping WMA's London operations; and ironically, he led the charge to trim some fat from Morris's bloated ranks (as have most agencies).

GEOFFREY SANFORD

The Sanford-Gross Agency
1015 Gayley Ave.
Suite 301
Los Angeles, CA 90024
Phone: (310) 208-2100
Fax: (310) 208-6704

A highly respected literary agent, Stanford, along with partner Brad Gross, found ways to work with other major agencies rather than see their boutique lit shop slowly emptied by them. Among those Sanford represents are scribes Nicholas Kazan (*Fallen*, *Matilda*) and Richard Price (*Ransom*, *Sea of Love*) and director Ron Shelton (*Bull Durham*, *White Men Can't Jump*). In addition to close ties with such powerhouses as Creative Artists Agency, which often packages its A-list actors and directors around screenplays by Sanford's clients, there is also an alliance with the Broder, Kurland, Webb & Uffner agency, a television dynamo, whereby Sanford-Gross consults on feature deals.

JOAN SCOTT

Founder/Partner
Writers & Artists Agency
924 Westwood Blvd.
Suite 900
Los Angeles, CA 90024
Phone: (323) 824-6300
Fax: (323) 824-6343

For the past thirty years, Joan Scott has overseen and maintained a successful mid-sized, full-service agency in one of the most competitive sectors of the entertainment business—no small feat. Though she recently relinquished some of the daily oversight of the agency—having appointed L.A. agents Norman Aladjem and Marti Blumenthal, along with Gotham head William Craver, to oversee the bi-coastal firm—she continues to be on the front line of new signings and active in the day-to-day administrative aspects of the company. Scott is one of the few female heads of a full-service agency, and over the course of her career, has discovered actors such as Henry Winkler, James Caan, and Elizabeth McGovern. Though the agency is often the target of poaching by larger firms, W&A has managed to keep and build careers for such actors as William H. Macy (*Fargo*), James Gandolfini (*The Sopranos*), Brendan Gleeson (*The General*), Shawn Wayans (*The Wayans Bros.*), and Hope Davis (*Daytrippers*). Other clients include directors Herb Ross (*Steel Magnolias*) and Nick Castle (*Mr. Wrong*). The percenter also repped the legit production *Rent* and its late creator, Jonathan Larson.

NICK STEVENS AND JOHN LESHER

Partners
United Talent Agency

As members of UTA's thirteen-person management team, John Lesher and Nick Stevens are two of the more highly regarded and top revenue generators for the agency. While neither is a consumate schmoozer or considerably press-savvy, they are respected agents in the film world, adept at taking breaking talent and moving them into

NICK STEVENS AND JOHN LESHER (CON'T)

9560 Wilshire Blvd.
Suite 500
Beverly Hills, CA 90212
Phone: (310) 273-6700
Fax: (310) 247-1111

the big leagues. Both have been with the agency since its inception in 1991, and both have weathered the bumpy ride from upstart to problem-riddled company to its present manifestation as a relatively stable, mid-sized percentery. Lesher, a Harvard grad and co-head of UTA's motion picture literary department (with Dan Aloni and Jeremy Zimmer), handles such rising filmmakers as Paul Thomas Anderson (*Boogie Nights*), David O. Russell (*Spanking the Monkey*), Ben Stiller (*The Cable Guy*), and producer/writer Judd Apatow (*The Cable Guy*). And Stevens, who oversees UTA's talent department, is the point-man for $20 million player Jim Carrey as well as for Vince Vaughn, among others. While the agency has lost Sandra Bullock and her $12 million paydays, Stevens's purview expanded with addition of former ICM talent agent Tracey Jacobs, who brought with her such clients as Johnny Depp, Jennifer Jason Leigh, Joan Cusack, and Vincent D'Onofrio. UTA also has brought into the fold such comers as Liz Hurley (*EDtv*) and Jim Caveziel (*The Thin Red Line*).

3 ARTS ENTERTAINMENT

Erwin Stoff, Howard Klein, and Michael Rotenberg
Partners

Led by partners Erwin Stoff, Howard Klein, and Michael Rotenberg, 3 Arts Entertainment has emerged as one of the major management/production firms in Hollywood, boasting a roster of clients that includes actors Keanu Reeves, Jennifer Aniston, Chris Rock, Mike Myers, and Salma Hayek, and writer/directors Mike Judge (TV's *King of the Hill* and *Office Space*) and Todd Solondz (*Happiness*). Over the years, and

3 ARTS ENTERTAINMENT (CON'T)
9460 Wilshire Blvd.
Beverly Hills, CA 90212
Phone: (310) 888-3200
Fax: (310) 888-3210

with varying results, 3 Arts has managed to leverage these talent relationships into TV and film production pacts with networks like CBS and studios such as 20th Century Fox. Though the firm does not develop material internally, 3 Arts, like most high-powered management companies, does command producing fees and credit as the price for putting their top clients in film projects—for which their actual producerial roles are negligible. Among the projects 3 Arts' principals have "produced" or exec produced are *National Lampoon's Loaded Weapon I*; the Keanu Reeves–starrers *Bill and Ted's Bogus Journey*, *Feeling Minnesota*, *Chain Reaction*, *Devil's Advocate*, and *The Matrix*, Judge's *Office Space*, and the Aniston vehicle *Picture Perfect*. As testimony to the demand for its clients, 3 Arts currently is involved with at least thirty feature projects (in varying stages of development) around Hollywood.

JIM WIATT

President/Co-CEO
William Morris Agency
151 El Camino Dr.
Beverly Hills, CA 90212
Phone: (310) 859-4000
Fax: (310) 859-4462

In August 1999, former ICM co-chairman and co-CEO Jim Wiatt moved to the William Morris Agency, taking the dual posts of president and co-CEO, and supplanting president Arnold Rifkin. Among the clients who joined Wiatt at William Morris were actors Eddie Murphy, Sylvester Stallone and Tim Allen, directors Nora Ephron, Penny Marshall, Richard Donner and Renny Harlin and writer Joe Eszterhas. At WMA, Wiatt serves on the board of directors and shares oversight of all areas of the agency and its worldwide operations. Wiatt signed a five-year pact and received a signing bonus as well as a base salary well above the $1.5 million he was receiving from ICM. But unlike ICM, Wiatt will not be an owner of the company and will likely have less managerial autonomy than he had at ICM, where he reported only to ICM chairman and CEO Jeff Berg. A well-connected, raconteur, Wiatt has been hailed by his staffers for being acessible, funny and the one who can explain the often Byzantine relationship structure of the industry. "But get on his bad side and you might as well not exist," says a former ICM agent.

DAVE WIRTSCHAFTER

Senior Literary Agent
International Creative Management
8942 Wilshire Blvd.
Beverly Hills, CA 90211
Phone: (310) 550-4000
Fax: (310) 550-4100

A true behind-the-scenes player, Wirtschafter is a virtual mystery man to the Hollywood press. His lack of time in the limelight hasn't diminished the respect he garners from both junior and senior colleagues, who view him as a possible future head for the agency. His power base at ICM is secure, provided he doesn't leave for another percentery or the management side, as were the rumors rampant in 1998 when he was passed over for the prexy slots given to Ed Limato and TV department head Nancy Josephson. Regardless of his internal political battles, Wirtschafter is heralded as one of the town's premier lit agents, boasting a client list that includes directors and writers Larry and Andy Wachowski (the WaTK bros.) (*The Matrix*), Carl Franklin (*One True Thing*), Wayne Wang

(*Anywhere but Here*), and Doug McGrath (*Emma*), as well as actress Winona Ryder. Before joining ICM in 1986, Wirtschafter worked even more behind the scenes, as a business affairs exec at rival Creative Artists Agency.

RICK YORN AND JULIE SILVERMAN YORN

Managers and Founding Partners

Artists Management Group
9465 Wilshire Blvd.
Beverly Hills, CA 90212
Phone: (310) 860-8000
Fax: (310) 271-9753

Rick Yorn and sister-in-law Julie Silverman Yorn were at the center of one of Hollywood's most heated executive shuffles of the past few years. Just a few months after being promoted to co-presidents of management/production firm Industry Entertainment, the two young managers ankled the company to establish rival banner Artists Mangement Group with former CAA chieftain Michael Ovitz.

Ovitz offered equity stakes in the company and a chance to build something from scratch; and the Yorns (whose combined client list includes Leonardo DiCaprio, Minnie Driver, Samuel L. Jackson, Cameron Diaz, Benicio Del Toro, Edward Burns, Matt Dillon, Lauren Holly, Marisa Tomei, and Ted Demme) brought Ovitz, who needed a high-profile, effective return to the business after a string of missteps, instant "oomph." Despite a habit of not returning non-clients' phone calls, those Yorn handles say he is a great listener, who doesn't try to impose his will or ambitions on them, and, unlike most of the yes-men in Hollywood, doesn't shy away from expressing his point of view. Silverman Yorn is regarded as a top-notch manager who essentially keeps the trains running at AMG.

Both Yorns, who are generally well liked, have been shell-shocked by the amount of press attention and number of new enemies who have cropped up since they teamed with Ovitz.

SCRIBES
(Screenwriters)

ATTANASIO, Paul · BASS, Ronald · CLANCY, Tom · CRICHTON, Michael · EPHRON, Delia · ESZTERHAS, Joe · FRANK, Scott · GOLDMAN, William · GRISHAM, John · HELGELAND, Brian · HENSLEIGH, Jonathan · JOHNSON, Mark Steven · KAZAN, Nicholas · KING, Stephen · KOEPP, David · MAMET, David · MANDEL, Babaloo, and Lowell Ganz · OEDEKERK, Steve · PRICE, Richard · ROSS, Gary · ROTH, Eric · SAYLES, John · TALLY, Ted · TOWNE, Robert · WALLACE, Randall · WHEDON, Joss · WILLIAMSON, Kevin · ZAILLIAN, Steven

SCRIBES

(Screenwriters)

Since even before "talkies" crept into theaters, writers have languished on the bottom of the cinema totem pole, with the livelihood and careers of the rest of Hollywood teetering on their hunched shoulders. Though they have been relegated to anonymity and disrespect over the years, anyone who makes his or her living in the film business is well aware that the scribes' work is perhaps the most essential in the process, and without them Hollywood would likely grind to a halt. No longer "schmucks with Underwoods," as Jack Warner once blithely referred to them, screenwriters today earn more than their predecessors ever dreamed, and many, particularly those on this list, have more say in the creative process than their forerunners and the rest of their contemporaries. Unlike the studio wage slaves immortalized in *Sunset Avenue*, today's power scribes enjoy such financial rewards as seven-figure paydays, profit participation, production bonuses, and studio term deals, as well as opportunities to produce and direct. And in this age of vertically integrated media conglomerates, they are often afforded other outlets for their material, including TV, the Internet, and publishing. Having made their bones as capable scribes, when these writers sign on to a project, their names actually lend a certain prestige that, used as the core of a "package," can propel a project to the next level, attracting an A-list actor or director.

In 1999, Sony broke new ground (much to the chagrin of competing studios) by inking a landmark deal with thirty-one individual writers and writer teams that promise to pay 2 percent of a pic's gross receipts, in all media, in perpetuity and 1 percent when the credit is shared with another writer or writers. To qualify, the scribes must have earned at least $750,000 as a front-end payment for a feature, sold a spec for at least $1 million, or received a nomination for an Academy Award or Writers Guild of America Award. The Sony deal was significant not only because it gave screenwriters a credibility boost but also because as studios' resistance to give gross points to directors and producers has withered over the years, they have been more resolute when it came to not allowing scribes access to this rarefied pay plan, which was once generally reserved for top stars. In the past, screenwriters were less successful in getting the perk because they usually worked on a script-by-script basis and tended to move from studio to studio. Needless to say, while the Sony list (which includes several of the following writers) was highly subjective and made up of scribes the studio consistently employs, its creation of this pay scale established a quasi-A-list among Hollywood writers. And although several writers on the following list were not part of the Sony roster (some by choice), you can be sure that all of them qualify and most, if not all, earn well above $750,000 for their work and have been gross players for some time.

PAUL ATTANASIO

Heel & Toe Films
Paramount Pictures
5555 Melrose Ave.
Los Angeles, CA 90038
Phone: (323) 960-4591
Fax: (323) 960-4592
Repped by:
Creative Artists Agency

In July 1998, Attanasio, the Oscar-nominated screenwriter of *Quiz Show* and *Donnie Brasco*, and his wife and producing partner, Katie Jacobs, inked a two-year deal with Paramount. The stated mission of their Heel & Toe Films is to develop and produce feature films, some of which Attanasio will direct, while creating a nurturing environment for other writers. Attanasio, a former *Washington Post* film critic, first gained attention for penning the pilot for the NBC drama series *Homicide: Life on the Street*, the gritty, long-running cop show produced by Barry Levinson. Levinson later hired Attanasio to write *Disclosure*, the successful feature thriller based on Michael Crichton's bestseller. Before settling at Par, Jacobs was partnered for two years with Gail Mutrux at Fox 2000, where the pair produced the Vince Vaughn–starrer *Cool, Dry Place*. Gail's other production credits include the comedies *Getting Even with Dad* and *Fatal Instinct* for MGM, and Alan J. Pakula's thriller *Consenting Adults* for Disney.

RONALD BASS

c/o Creative Artists Agency
9830 Wilshire Blvd.
Beverly Hills, CA 90212
Phone: (310) 288-4545
Fax: (310) 288-4800

Ron Bass seems to have a finger in just about every pie in Hollywood. A former Harvard-trained industry lawyer, he is an Oscar-winning writer (*Rain Man*), whose numerous credits include *Stepmom*, *When a Man Loves a Woman*, *Dangerous Minds*, *Entrapment*, *Sleeping with the Enemy*, *Gardens of Stone*, *The Joy Luck Club*, *Waiting to Exhale*, and *My Best Friend's Wedding*, to name a few. Bass has parlayed that screenwriting success into a producing deal at Sony Pictures Entertainment, where he was part of a five-man squad of penmen who formulated the landmark contract with Sony, initially giving thirty-one select writers 2 percent of a film's gross—the first time that writers, as a group, had been contractually entitled to a percentage of the gross. But a more interesting aspect of his career is his "Ronettes," staff writers he retains to help cobble together the scripts he seems to churn out so effortlessly—hence, the great variety of themes.

TOM CLANCY

c/o William Morris Agency
1325 Avenue of the Americas
New York, NY 10019

In addition to the author's worldwide popularity (hardcover versions of his books routinely sell in the millions) and the fierce loyalty of his fan base, Clancy's obsession with whiz-bang military hardware and insider's knowledge of the

TOM CLANCY (CON'T)

Phone: (212) 586-5100

Fax: (212) 246-3583

Washington power base make his books unbeatable source material for film and TV. Three of Clancy's Jack Ryan novels—*The Hunt for Red October*, *Patriot Games*, and *Clear and Present Danger*—form the basis of one of Paramount Pictures' most successful franchises. Released over a period of just four years (1990–1994), the high-tech espionage thrillers accounted for nearly $600 million in worldwide grosses, and countless more in ancillary sales. But in the early '90s Clancy had a high-profile falling out with Par over creative decisions, and a rapprochement was slow in coming. In 1996, Clancy inked a five-year miniseries and series TV deal with ABC, for which he exec produced the futuristic 1999 telepic *Netforce*.

MICHAEL CRICHTON

c/o Creative Artists Agency

9830 Wilshire Blvd.

Beverly Hills, CA 90212

Phone: (310) 288-4545

Fax: (310) 288-4800

Crichton is the T-Rex of novelists when it comes to blockbuster movie adaptations, and one of the few writers whose name alone can be counted on to sell tickets. *Jurassic Park* and its first sequel devoured a global theatrical gross of $1.5 billion and became one of Universal's biggest properties in terms of everything from merchandise to theme park rides. Amblin's *Twister*, which Crichton and his wife, Ann-Marie Martin, scripted, whipped up over $490 million worldwide for Warner Bros. and Universal, while the film version of Crichton's *Disclosure* uncovered another $212 million for WB. Perhaps the best measure of his popularity is the fact that even the critically panned *Congo* grossed $80 million in the U.S., largely on the strength of Crichton's post-*Jurassic* juice. Of course, no one's perfect: The costly Barry Levinson–helmed undersea adventure *Sphere* sank without a trace, for example. An alumnus of Harvard Medical School, Crichton gained attention with the sci-fi bestseller *The Andromeda Strain* before segueing into a brief career as a director. After the campy futuristic thriller *Westworld*, he followed up with *Coma* and *The Great Train Robbery* before hitting a career sag in the mid-'80s. Things began to look up in a big way when the author turned his attention to dinosaurs. In addition to his big-screen successes, Crichton wrote the pilot for WB and NBC's highly rated *ER*, a show that is credited with resuscitating the hour-long drama form in the mid-'90s. Crichton is intensely private and rarely makes the rounds of Hollywood dinner parties or industry functions, preferring to divide his time between homes in Santa Monica and Kauai.

DELIA EPHRON

c/o Creative Artists Agency
9830 Wilshire Blvd.
Beverly Hills, CA 90212
Phone: (310) 288-4545
Fax: (310) 288-4800

Rushing through a door opened by her older sister (*Sleepless in Seattle* and *You've Got Mail* director Nora Ephron), Delia Ephron has been working steadily as a Hollywood screenwriter for over a decade. With Nora, Delia has written screenplays for *You've Got Mail*, *Michael*, *Mixed Nuts*, and *This Is My Life*, and on her own she contributed to the dud *Brenda Starr*, for which she used the pseudonym Jenny Wolkind. Delia also served as executive producer on *You've Got Mail*, *Michael*, and *Mixed Nuts*. Outside Hollywood, Ephron established herself as a journalist and author who has written such nonfiction tomes as *How to Eat Like a Child* and *Teenage Romance or How to Die of Embarrassment*, as well as the children's books *My Life (and Nobody Else's)* and *The Girl Who Changed the World*. With her first foray into adult fiction, the 1995 bestseller *Hanging Up*, Delia turned inward, basing the story on her own family. Columbia Pictures optioned the novel, which Delia adapted for Diane Keaton to direct and star in, along with Meg Ryan and Lisa Kudrow. Delia executive produced the pic, while Nora and Laurence Mark produced.

JOE ESZTERHAS

c/o William Morris Agency
151 El Camino Dr.
Beverly Hills, CA 90212
Phone: (310) 859-4000
Fax: (310) 859-4462

One of the scribes most closely associated with the high-flying spec screenplay market of the late '80s to mid-'90s, Eszterhas probably made more money and garnered more publicity than any other screenwriter of the decade. Between 1990 and 1997, he sold seven screenplays for advances of at least a million dollars each. Of those scripts, only one had been made as of mid-1999: the 1992 erotic thriller *Basic Instinct*, for which he commanded a $3 million payday. With the notable exception of blockbusters such as 1983's *Flashdance* and *Basic Instinct* a decade later, Eszterhas's box office track record offers no obvious explanation for his exorbitant paydays. His hits are far outnumbered by his clunkers, which include *Showgirls*, *Jade*, *Telling Lies in America*, and the disastrous Hollywood sendup *An Alan Smithee Film: Burn, Hollywood, Burn*, which earned a paltry $46,000 domestically, despite cameos by a raft of Hollywood A-listers. However, because he is synonymous with million-dollar paydays (and because he has developed that rare status for writers, celebrity), anytime he writes a script, you can be sure that virtually every studio will want to read it, if not bid for it.

SCOTT FRANK

c/o Creative Artists Agency
9830 Wilshire Blvd.
Beverly Hills, CA 90212
Phone: (310) 288-4545
Fax: (310) 288-4800

Frank got his start with the critically acclaimed but commercially stunted 1991 drama *Little Man Tate*, which he wrote while working as a bartender in L.A. Subsequent credits included the pitch for what became *Dead Again*, a rewrite of *Malice*, and his break-out adaptation of Elmore Leonard's *Get Shorty*. After an artistically barren period, churning out uncredited fender-and-body work on screenplays that ranged from the animated *Quest for Camelot* to *Saving Private Ryan* to *Entrapment*, Frank found further acclaim with his Oscar-nominated adaptation of Leonard's *Out of Sight*. That pic propelled him into the upper echelon of A-list scribes. As testament to his status, he recently was brought in to rewrite *Minority Report*, for the first collaboration between director Steven Spielberg and star Tom Cruise. Frank also has moved into producing with his Arroyo Pictures, which has a first-look deal with Universal-based Jersey Films.

WILLIAM GOLDMAN

c/o Creative Artists Agency

Despite Hollywood's overwhelming obsession with youth, Goldman, who turns sixty-nine in the year 2000, still sits atop the highest peak of Hollywood writers. The gurulike scribe has over

WILLIAM GOLDMAN (CON'T)

9830 Wilshire Blvd.
Beverly Hills, CA 90212
Phone: (310) 288-4545
Fax: (310) 288-4800

twenty-five screen credits to his name—as well as numerous uncredited rewrites—with recent examples including *The General's Daughter*, *Absolute Power*, *Maverick*, and *Misery*. Goldman started out in the early '60s as a novelist before bursting onto the Hollywood scene with the seminal 1969 neo-western *Butch Cassidy and the Sundance Kid*. He followed that with such '70s classics as *The Stepford Wives*, *Marathon Man*, and *All the President's Men*, and later the 1987 comedy adventure *The Princess Bride*, based on his bestselling fairy tale parody. Among Hollywood insiders Goldman's most frequently quoted line is his take on the unpredi-ability of the movie business: "Nobody knows anything."

JOHN GRISHAM

c/o The Gernert Company
136 East 57th St.
New York, NY 10022
Phone: (212) 838-7777
Fax: (212) 838-6020

A former small-town Mississippi attorney turned bestselling author of legal thrillers, John Grisham has had enormous success in the film industry as well. He was on his way to becoming a brand name with the 1993 big-screen adaptation of *The Firm*, directed by Sydney Pollack and starring Tom Cruise as a virtuous young attorney working for a law firm run by the mob. Since then, five more films have been made from Grisham potboilers, including *A Time to Kill* (1996), *The Pelican Brief* (1993), *The Client* (1994), and *The Chamber* (1996). Grisham took home a reported $3.75 million for the screen rights to *The Chamber*, and he received $6 million—plus casting approval—for the rights to *A Time to Kill*. Attempting to assume greater control of his material, Grisham wrote and produced the Francis Ford Coppola–helmed *The Rainmaker* in 1997. After a reported $8 million rights sale to Warner Bros. for his *Runaway Jury* fell apart, Grisham issued a moratorium on selling his books to Hollywood because he felt there was a glut of his properties in the marketplace. He had little success with his first original screenplay, *The Gingerbread Man* (1998), which was directed by Robert Altman, who rewrote Grisham's script, leaving the scribe with only a story credit.

BRIAN HELGELAND

c/o Missy Malkin
Malkin Management
465 South Beverly Dr.
Third Floor
Beverly Hills, CA 90212
Phone: (310) 226-2555
Fax: (310) 226-2550

Though he is one of the highest-paid writers in Hollywood, Brian Helgeland's career has been a roller coaster of hits and misses. A former New England commercial fisherman, Helgeland made a career switch in 1986 and came to Hollywood for another fishing expedition: screenwriting. His first jobs in the business included work on such horror pics as the Renny Harlin–helmed *A Nightmare on Elm Street 4: The Dream Master* and Robert Englund's *976-EVIL*. Helgeland received his first solo screenwriting credit for the 1992 pic *Highway to Hell*, before collaborating on a series of films with producer-director Richard Donner, including the thriller *Assassins* in 1995, and *Conspiracy Theory* in 1997, and *Lethal Weapon 4* in 1998. He gained critical notoriety as co-writer and co-producer of Curtis Hanson's 1997 take on James Ellroy's noir tale, *L.A. Confidential*. He followed that Oscar-nominated screenplay with the failed futuristic drama

The Postman, which Kevin Costner directed and starred in. His working relationship with Mel Gibson probably ended for good with the 1999 film *Payback*, which was to mark Helgeland's directing debut. Word soon leaked out that Gibson, a producer of the film, and Paramount reshot several scenes and edited the film without his input, though Helgeland does receive screenplay and director credits.

JONATHAN HENSLEIGH

Valhalla Entertainment
5555 Melrose Ave.
Lubitsch Annex
Suite 119
Hollywood, CA 90038
Phone: (323) 956-8601
Fax: (323) 862-1101
Repped by: Endeavor Agency

Jonathan Hensleigh made his name writing or inspiring such big-budget actioners as *Armageddon*, *Virus*, *The Saint*, *Con Air*, *Jumanji*, and *Die Hard with a Vengeance*. Married to producer Gale Anne Hurd, Hensleigh is planning on making his directing debut with Universal's comic book adaptation *Hulk*, which Hurd will produce—although the project has stumbled in the starting blocks because of its pocket-draining budget. In the meantime, he's penning or rewriting such screenplays as *Jumanji 2*, *Red Tails*, *Hickock and Cody*, *Golf in the Kingdom*, *Ghost Rider*, and *Captain Blood*.

MARK STEVEN JOHNSON

Horseshoe Bay Productions
710 Wilshire Blvd.
Suite 600
Santa Monica, CA 90401

Mark Steven Johnson, with five screenplays to his name, has leapfrogged over hurdles the industry often puts in front of scribes. He wrote his first project, *Grumpy Old Men*, when he was a clock-punching receptionist for Orion Pictures in the studio's final days, basing it on old men he knew from his Minnesota hometown. Sporting

MARK STEVEN JOHNSON (CON'T)
Phone: (310) 587-0787
Fax: (310) 899-4259
Repped by: William Morris Agency

Jack Lemmon and Walter Matthau as the irascible leads, the film was a box office surprise. It led to *Grumpier Old Men*, *Big Bully*, *Jack Frost*, and *Simon Birch*, the last of which Johnson also directed. Now one of the top rewrite men in town, he's tackling several projects that he's also producing, including *Titanic Thompson*, *Love on Trial*, *In My Shoes*, and *Fanatics*.

NICHOLAS KAZAN

c/o The Sanford-Gross Agency
1015 Gayley Ave.
Suite 301
Los Angeles, CA 90024
Phone: (310) 208-2100
Fax: (310) 208-6704

In a business based almost entirely on relationships, Nick Kazan has managed the unmanageable. As a screenwriter, he's made the industry forget that he's the son of acclaimed director and blacklist-era stool pigeon Elia Kazan (who was the recipient of a controversial Lifetime Achievement Award at the 1999 Oscar ceremony). For Nick Kazan, the road has never been all that easy. The writer carved out a career with edgy, terse, darkly funny scripts like *At Close Range*, *Patty Hearst*, *Reversal of Fortune*, *Mobsters*, *Dream Lover*, *Homegrown*, and *Fallen*, the last starring Denzel Washington. With wife Robin Swicord, he went on to pen Roald Dahl's *Matilda* for Danny DeVito and Rhea Perlman.

STEPHEN KING

c/o Creative Artists Agency
9830 Wilshire Blvd.
Beverly Hills, CA 90212
Phone: (310) 288-4545

This almost supernaturally prolific novelist is one of just a handful of scribes whose clout and name recognition command possessory credit above the title (e.g., *Stephen King's Thinner*). King has racked up an astounding fifty-plus film and TV credits since the 1976 release of Brian

STEPHEN KING (CON'T)

Fax: (310) 288-4800

De Palma's *Carrie*—based on King's first published novel—launched his career. King's writings have provided source material for everything from B-movie horror franchises like *Children of the Corn* and its brood of sequels to upscale offerings including *The Shining* (1980), *Stand by Me* (1986), *Misery* (1990), *The Shawshank Redemption* (1994), *Dolores Claiborne* (1995), and *The Green Mile* (1999). Filmmakers inspired by King run the gamut from the nightmarishly surreal David Cronenberg, who made his feature debut on the King adaptation *The Dead Zone*, to Rob Reiner, who directed both *Stand by Me* and *Misery* (and named his production company, Castle Rock, after King's fictional Maine town). While he lives a relatively quiet life in New England, far from the bright lights of Hollywood, King's not a complete outsider, having exec produced several TV miniseries, appeared in over a dozen movies (most notably *Creepshow*) and even directed a feature—albeit a total bomb—the 1986 horror actioner *Maximum Overdrive*.

DAVID KOEPP

c/o Hofflund/Polone
Management
9465 Wilshire Blvd.
Suite 820
Beverly Hills, CA 90212
Phone: (310) 859-1971
Fax: (310) 859-7250

Embodying the dreams of every screenwriter wannabe who ever ate breakfast at L.A.'s Farmers' Market, this Wisconsin native moved with velociraptor speed from total obscurity to screenplay credits on three of the biggest blockbusters of the mid-'90s. After graduating from UCLA Film School, Koepp made his feature debut in 1988, producing and writing the indie drama *Apartment Zero*, based on his own play.

He followed that with *Bad Influence*, a Curtis Hanson–helmed psychological thriller starring James Spader and Rob Lowe. In 1992, he landed a contract writing gig at Universal, where with Martin Donovan he co-wrote the supernatural comedy *Death Becomes Her* for director Robert Zemeckis. It wasn't long after Zemeckis introduced him to his pal Steven Spielberg that Koepp was brought on to adapt Michael Crichton's *Jurassic Park*, along with the bestselling author. The effects-driven dinosaur pic is hardly known for richly drawn characters or insightful dialogue, but with nearly $920 million in worldwide ticket sales, Koepp's participation was more than enough to propel the then thirty-year-old scribe onto the A-List. He went on to pen the 1994 pic *The Paper*, along with his brother and *Time* magazine editor Stephen Koepp, and 1996's *Mission: Impossible*, which despite a story line many found indecipherable, grossed over $450 million worldwide. Koepp made his feature directing debut on 1996's *The Trigger Effect*—which had little effect on the box office—before re-teaming with Spielberg for the 1997 sequel *The Lost World: Jurassic Park*.

DAVID MAMET

c/o Howard Rosenstone
Rosenstone/Wender Agency
3 East 48th St.
New York, NY 10017
Phone: (212) 832-8330

One of the twentieth century's best playwrights, David Mamet has had only so-so success as a screenwriter in comparison. Still, he raises the bar so high as a playwright that his film work can't be ignored. He's able to write and direct fascinating films that are more Chinese puzzles than linear expositions—*Spanish Prisoner*, *House of Games*,

DAVID MAMET (CON'T)
Fax: (212) 759-4524

Things Change, *Homicide*, and *The Winslow Boy*—as well as scripts he simply writes, like his first produced screenplay, *The Postman Always Rings Twice*, for Bob Rafelson; his play *Glengarry Glen Ross*, for James Foley; *The Untouchables*, for Brian De Palma; *The Edge*, for Lee Tamahori; and his Academy Award–nominated *The Verdict*, for Sidney Lumet. While he is known for his irascibility, Mamet is also known for the compassion he exudes for his actors (Alec Baldwin seems to deliver his best work in Mamet-scripted roles) when he's directing. Scatological, to be sure, but if Mamet is writing it, then it has a point and smart dialogue. And if not outright sexist, it's usually male to a fault.

BABALOO MANDEL AND LOWELL GANZ

c/o Creative Artists Agency
9830 Wilshire Blvd.
Beverly Hills, CA 90212
Phone: (310) 288-4545
Fax: (310) 288-4800

Mandel and Ganz: two names that for nearly a quarter century have rarely been uttered separately in Hollywood. This enduring writing partnership began in the mid-'70s, when Mandel was a joke writer for standups including Joan Rivers, and Ganz had a staff writer job on *The Odd Couple*. The pair first teamed on the long-running sitcom *Laverne and Shirley*. (Ganz reportedly nicknamed Mandel, whose real name is Marc, "Babaloo" after a character in Philip Roth's risqué novel *Portnoy's Complaint*.) The two are closely associated with both Brian Grazer and Ron Howard's Imagine Entertainment, with which they collaborated on *Night Shift*, *Splash*, *Gung Ho*, *Parenthood*, and *EDtv*, and also with Billy Crystal, for whom they wrote *City Slickers* 1 & 2, *Mr. Saturday Night*,

Forget Paris, and *Father's Day*. Other credits include the Penny Marshall–helmed *A League of Their Own*. Known as family guys, they still live in the outré San Fernando Valley. In 1997, Mandel briefly broke ranks to pen *Joe's Dream* for Village Roadshow Pictures.

STEVE OEDEKERK

O Entertainment
31878 Camino Capistrano
Suite 101
San Juan Capistrano, CA 92675
Phone: (949) 443-3222
Fax: (949) 443-3223
Repped by:
William Morris Agency

Overcoming an unspectacular early career as a standup comic and TV sketch comedy writer (*In Living Color*) during the late '80s, Steve Oedekerk came into his own in the mid-'90s when he made his feature debut as writer-director on the Jim Carrey–starrer *Ace Ventura: When Nature Calls*, the sequel to *Ace Ventura: Pet Detective*. That film vaulted him into the upper echelon of comedy scribes. Following *Ace Ventura*, Oedekerk snared plum writing assignments for such pics as *The Nutty Professor*, *Patch Adams*, and *The Incredible Mr. Limpet* (which he was to direct, but later dropped out). Oedekerk also wrote and directed the 1997 buddy comedy *Nothing to Lose*, which starred Martin Lawrence and Tim Robbins.

RICHARD PRICE

c/o Sanford-Gross Agency
1015 Gayley Ave.
Suite 301
Los Angeles, CA 90024

Price's novels excel at capturing the gritty lives and terse patois of cops, petty criminals, and working-class heroes who inhabit the decaying urban housing projects and blue-collar suburbs surrounding Manhattan. Born in the Bronx in 1949, Price has enjoyed a symbiotic relationship with Hollywood ever since his first novel, *The Wanderers*, was

RICHARD PRICE (CON'T)

Phone: (310) 208-2100
Fax: (310) 208-6704

adapted for the big screen in 1979. He later found success with original screenplays for the Martin Scorsese–helmed sequel to *The Hustler*, *The Color of Money* (1986), which earned him an Oscar nom, and the sexy crime thriller *Sea of Love* (1989). He collaborated again with Scorsese, whom he credits as an early inspiration, on the "Life Lessons" segment of the 1989 anthology pic *New York Stories*. Price's career stalled slightly in the early '90s, when the noir remakes *Night and the City* (1992) and *Kiss of Death* (1995) fared poorly at the box office, as did the critically acclaimed 1993 mob comedy, *Mad Dog and Glory*, which Price wrote and exec produced. But he hit the jackpot with *Clockers*, when Universal stepped up with a reported $1.9 million payday for the movie rights and his screen adaptation of the novel about crack dealers in a New Jersey housing project. Scorsese was at one point attached to helm the pic, but when he dropped out, it was directed—and rewritten—by Spike Lee. The pic nodded off with a $13 million domestic gross. In the late '90s, Price enjoyed a productive and lucrative relationship with book-savvy producer Scott Rudin, for whom he did screenplay work on *Ransom* and *Shaft*, and for whom Paramount bought rights to Price's crime novel *Freedomland*.

GARY ROSS

Larger Than Life Productions
100 Universal City Plaza
Building 489

Gary Ross has only five screenplays to his credit, three of which launched him to the bigtime: *Big*, which was written with Anne Spielberg and starred Tom Hanks; the Oscar-nominated, solo effort *Dave*, starring Kevin Kline and Sigourney

GARY ROSS (CON'T)
Universal City, CA 91608
Phone: (818) 777-4004
Fax: (818) 866-5677
Repped by:
Creative Artists Agency

Weaver; and his directorial debut, *Pleasantville*. Armed with these credits (he is a credited writer on *Mr. Baseball* and *Lassie* as well), Ross has ventured further up the Hollywood food chain, claiming spots as producer and director as well as scribe. Other screenplay work has involved passes at *The Flintstones* (uncredited) and *Inspector Gadget*. He now has an overall deal at Universal with partner Jane Sindell that allows him to make the films that interest him. Though *Pleasantville* generally gleaned decent reviews, it didn't make much money for New Line Cinema. So the studios are watching Ross a little more closely, but generally he can pick and choose what he wants to do. Another Hollywood legacy, Ross is the son of screenwriter Arthur Ross, who was nominated for an Oscar for his screenplay of *Brubaker*.

ERIC ROTH

c/o Creative Artists Agency
9830 Wilshire Blvd.
Beverly Hills, CA 90212
Phone: (310) 288-4545
Fax: (310) 288-4800

Roth's presence on the Hollywood A-list really comes down to two words: *Forrest Gump*. Aside from that blockbuster, which grossed roughly $680 million worldwide and earned Roth an Oscar for Adapted Screenplay, the scribe has had a far from prolific career. In the quarter of a century since his first feature, the Robert Mulligan–directed *The Nickel Ride,* Roth penned scripts for just six films, including *The Concorde—Airport '79* (1979), the Cher-starrer *Suspect* (1987), the Henry Winkler–helmed *Memories of Me* (1988), and the romantic drama *Mr. Jones* (1993). Roth is also credited, along with Brian Helgeland, with adapting David Brin's post-apocalyptic novel *The Postman*, a colossal box office and critical disaster in 1997, and the more successful adaptation, along with Richard LaGravanese, of Nicholas Evans's novel *The Horse Whisperer* for director-star Robert Redford.

JOHN SAYLES

c/o Paradigm Talent & Literary Agency
10100 Santa Monica Blvd.
Twenty-fifth Floor
Los Angeles, CA 90067
Phone: (310) 277-4400
Fax: (310) 277-7820

John Sayles has always skirted by with a Sundance sensibility, but draws paychecks (for his writing services) from a studio bank account. While known by a wider audience as an acclaimed director who makes films about diverse, and wildly uncommercial topics, he'll also do uncredited rewrites and script polishes (for as much as $1 million a pop) on studio films. This gives him oodles of cash to pay for his critically lauded but mostly uncommercial films like *Eight Men Out* and *Men with Guns*. From his New Jersey base he has ventured out to write and direct such screen gems as *Brother from Another Planet*, *Passion Fish*, *Lone Star*, *City of Hope*, *Lianna* and his '70s take on '60s college grads, *Return of the Secaucus Seven*. Sayles garnered Oscar nominations for his screenplays for *Passion Fish* and *Lone Star*, but went home empty-handed in both instances. His one venture into TV, *Shannon's Deal*, was uninspired, but he also has directed Bruce Springsteen's music videos, written novels in Spanish and won the MacArthur genius grant. His latest effort, *Limbo*, made it into competition at Cannes. But didn't win.

TED TALLY

c/o International Creative Management
8942 Wilshire Blvd.
Beverly Hills, CA 90211
Phone: (310) 550-4000
Fax: (310) 550-4100

An acclaimed screenwriter and playwright, Ted Tally hit the high point of his career in 1991 when he won an Academy Award for his adaptation of Thomas Harris's *The Silence of the Lambs*. Tally, an alum of Yale Drama School, first made a name for himself in the late '70s and '80s for his legit work, which included the Obie-winning *Terra Nova*. After a stint in TV in the early '80s (Tally adapted his 1978 off-Broadway play *Hooters* for the Playboy Channel), he segued to features in 1990 when he adapted, with Alvin Sargent, Glenn Savan's novel *White Palace*. Tally followed that with *The Silence of the Lambs* for director Jonathan Demme. Tally's subsequent credits—*The Juror*, starring Demi Moore and Alec Baldwin, and *Before and After*, starring Liam Neeson and Meryl Street—pale in comparison to *Lambs*. Nonetheless, Tally is an established force in the writing game, and is in hot demand by studios, particularly those wanting to adapt a piece of literature, for which he brings home more than $1 million.

ROBERT TOWNE

c/o Creative Artists Agency
9830 Wilshire Blvd.
Beverly Hills, CA 90212
Phone: (310) 288-4545
Fax: (310) 288-4800

Robert Towne is considered the gritty poet of '70s directors Francis Ford Coppola, Warren Beatty, Sam Peckinpah, Hal Ashby, Paul Schrader, Roman Polanski, and Sydney Pollack. He was responsible for such cleanly etched material as *The Last Detail*, *Bonnie and Clyde* (uncredited), *The Godfather* (just one scene, where Marlon Brando transfers power to Al Pacino), *Chinatown*, and *Shampoo*. His other screenplays include *Personal Best*,

Tequila Sunrise, *The Two Jakes*, *Days of Thunder*, *The Firm*, *Love Affair*, and *Without Limits*, which he directed. Towne was once tight with Jack Nicholson, but that relationship faded after *The Two Jakes* star fired him as a director on the *Chinatown* sequel. But he has remained close to producer Bob Evans and the wild '70s lifestyle the latter still upholds. His third screenplay to be nominated for an Oscar was *Greystoke: Legend of Tarzan,* originally credited to P. H. Vasak. P. H. Vasak turned out to be Towne's dog.

RANDALL WALLACE

c/o International Creative Management
8942 Wilshire Blvd.
Beverly Hills, CA 90211
Phone: (310) 550-4000
Fax: (310) 550-4100

Tennessee-born Randall Wallace is a former novelist, who during his salad years landed a job as an in-house writer/producer for Stephen Cannell Productions, where he worked on such short-lived TV series as *J.J. Starbuck*, *Sonny Spoon*, and *Broken Badges*. Seeds for his feature breakthrough were planted during a trip to Scotland, when Wallace discovered the legend of thirteenth-century revolutionary William Wallace, who fought against English rule. The legend became Wallace's 1995 Oscar-nominated screenplay for the film *Braveheart*, directed by and starring Mel Gibson. Wallace followed that by making his directorial debut, from his script, on the 1998 box office hit *The Man in the Iron Mask*, which starred Leonardo DiCaprio. A selective worker, Wallace has spent the last few years trying to get his WWII epic, *With Wings As Eagles*, before the cameras. He is likely to direct that pic for Paramount.

JOSS WHEDON

Mutant Enemy, Inc.
P.O. Box 900
Beverly Hills, CA 90213-0900
Phone: (310) 579-5180
Fax: (310) 579-5380

At a very young age, Joss Whedon became one of the highest-paid screenwriters in town, receiving $1.5 million from Columbia in 1994 for his spec *Afterlife* and $750,000 the year before for his spec *Suspension*. Whedon's other credits include the Oscar-nominated screenplay for Disney's *Toy Story*. He also did a production rewrite on *Twister* in 1995, and was hired to punch up the dialogue for Universal's big budget event pic *Waterworld*.

Whedon, a third-generation scripter, began his career as a story editor on ABC's *Roseanne*, where he wrote eight episodes during the show's second season. Whedon entered a new realm of industry elite with the success of his TV series *Buffy the Vampire Slayer*. That show led to a reported $16 million deal with 20th Century Fox film and TV divisions. Under the deal, Whedon writes, directs and produces all films generated by his company, and he executive produces all TV projects. Whedon's relationship with the studio dates back to the 1990 feature *Buffy the Vampire Slayer*. Whedon also wrote Fox's feature *Alien Resurrection*, and he did an uncredited production rewrite on the Fox hit *Speed* in 1994. Whedon and Fox Animation Studios are developing an animated musical feature film based on the legend of *Dracula*.

KEVIN WILLIAMSON

Outbanks Entertainment

If films by schlockmeister Roger Corman are offered up as inspiration for Peter Bogdonavich and James Cameron's generations of filmmakers, then Kevin Williamson is sure to become the muse for a whole new collective of future film-

KEVIN WILLIAMSON (CON'T)

8000 Sunset Blvd.
Third Floor
Los Angeles, CA 90046
Phone: (323) 654-3700
Fax: (323) 654-3797
Repped by: International Creative Management

makers who prefer *Halloween* over *Citizen Kane*. Williamson is credited with nearly single-handedly reviving the once moribund horror genre; and in the process becoming the millionaire Pied Piper of the Y and Z generations. With credits that include *Scream*, *Scream 2*, *I Know What You Did Last Summer*, *The Faculty,* and *Killing Mrs. Tingle* (released as *Teaching Mrs. Tingle*), Williamson took the stale teen exploitation films of the '70s and '80s and updated them with a '90s smirk. While much of his attention is focused on his TV series (*Dawson's Creek* and *Wasteland*), Williamson continues to churn out material under his multimillion-dollar film and TV production deal with Miramax/Dimension Films. Under the eight-figure deal, Williamson directed *Mrs. Tingle* (his helming debut from the first script he wrote) and penned *The Faculty* and the third installment of the *Scream* series.

STEVEN ZAILLIAN

c/o Harold Greene Agency
13900 Marquesas Way
Building C
Suite 83
Marina Del Rey, CA 90292
Phone: (310) 823-5393
Fax: (310) 821-7440

Steven Zaillian, who as an editor cut such films as *Breaker! Breaker!* and *Starhops*, has clearly risen to the elite inner circle of top screenwriters in Hollywood with such credits as *Awakenings*, the Oscar-winning *Schindler's List*, *The Falcon and the Snowman*, *Clear and Present Danger*, *Searching for Bobby Fischer*, and *A Civil Action* under his belt. And for a good chunk of change, he'll settle into uncredited rewrite work, as he did on *Amistad*, *Twister*, and *Saving Private Ryan*. As a director, he was able to grab attention from everyone but the audience for *Searching for Bobby Fischer*. And his sophomore effort, *A*

Civil Action, was well received by the critics, though it, too, had no box office juice. Still, the former film editor's at work on two projects: *The Duke of Deception*, which he'll write and direct, and an untitled Walter Winchell biopic for Martin Scorsese.

THESPS
(Actors)

BULLOCK, Sandra · CAGE, Nicolas · CARREY, Jim · CONNERY, Sean · COSTNER, Kevin · CRUISE, Tom · DE NIRO, Robert · DIAZ, Cameron · DICAPRIO, Leonardo · DOUGLAS, Michael · FORD, Harrison · FOSTER, Jodie · GIBSON, Mel · HANKS, Tom · HOFFMAN, Dustin · HUNT, Helen · JONES, Tommy Lee · MURPHY, Eddie · NICHOLSON, Jack · PALTROW, Gwyneth · PITT, Brad · REEVES, Keanu · ROBERTS, Julia · RYAN, Meg · SANDLER, Adam · SCHWARZENEGGER, Arnold · SMITH, Will · STALLONE, Sylvester · TRAVOLTA, John · WASHINGTON, Denzel · WILLIAMS, Robin · WILLIS, Bruce

THESPS

(Actors)

While the question of what makes a star a star is usually answered with vague statements—"I know one when I see one" or "They have to have that certain sparkle in their eye"—the one thing all of the following stars have in common (although to varying degrees) is their bankability. Each of their names lends an awareness or drawing power that translates to money in the bank for studios. And their attachment to a project in the early stages can make the difference between development hell and a green light. Often the expensive development process comes down to fine-tuning a script and attaching the right creative elements in an effort to attract one of these thesps—and if they pass, the projects are often downgraded or fall by the wayside.

In recent years Hollywood has undergone a major facelift, seen on screen with the arrival of several new A-list stars, who, because they attract audiences around the globe, now earn eight-figure paydays and wield enormous clout. On this list are many of the same faces that have consistently been putting "asses in the seats" for years, but a new generation is evident with the emergence of such young heavyweights as Will Smith, Leonardo DiCaprio, Nicolas Cage, Cameron Diaz, Adam Sandler, and Gwyneth Paltrow.

Though men continue to dominate the global box office, their distaff counterparts have made great strides in recent years to catch up on the salary front. For instance, Julia Roberts reportedly became the first femme to reach the vaunted $20 million per pic mark; and a few more, including Jodie Foster, Meg Ryan, and Sandra Bullock, are not far behind. And while studios cringe at the reality of another batch of $20 million players, they muffle their discomfort, insisting that these star salaries are merely insurance premiums and are worth the cost because with these A-listers on board, a film is less likely to sink in the global box office.

SANDRA BULLOCK

Fortis Films
8581 Santa Monica Blvd.
West Hollywood, CA 90069
Phone: (310) 659-4533
Fax: (310) 659-4373
Repped by:
Creative Artists Agency

As one of just a handful of female stars who can offer studios some guarantee of opening weekend muscle, Bullock's quote skyrocketed from $500,000 on *Speed* to over $10 million just a few years later. Spunky and likable in a girl-next-door way, Bullock has starred in such hits as *Demolition Man*, *Speed*, *A Time to Kill*, and *While You Were Sleeping*. Not just another pretty face, Bullock made her producing debut in collaboration with industry vet Lynda Obst on 20th Century Fox's *Hope Floats*. Fortis Films, Bullock's production company, inked a three-year first-look deal with Warner Bros. in 1997, and served as producer on the studio's moderately successful Fall 1998 release *Practical Magic*, in which Bullock starred with Nicole Kidman.

NICOLAS CAGE

Saturn Films
9000 Sunset Blvd.
Suite 911
West Hollywood, CA 90069
Phone: (310) 887-0900
Fax: (310) 248-2965
Repped by:
Creative Artists Agency

A member of both the $20-million-per-pic and the first-dollar gross participant clubs, Cage has emerged as one of Hollywood's top-paid stars. And he's justified his fat paychecks with consistent box office performance: With the 1998 release *City of Angels*, Cage had racked up five pics in a row with openings of $15 million or more. Once known mostly for dramatic roles as damaged outcasts in films like *Moonstruck* and *Leaving Las Vegas* (for which he won an acting Oscar), in the mid-'90s Cage transformed himself into an unlikely action hero, toplining in $100 million–grossing shoot-'em-ups such as *Con Air*, *The Rock*, and *Face/Off*. In 1999, Cage added producer to his résumé when his Saturn

Films banner announced it would make the $10 million indie pic *Shadow of the Vampire*.

JIM CARREY

c/o United Talent Agency
9560 Wilshire Blvd.
Suite 500
Beverly Hills, CA 90212
Phone: (310) 273-6700
Fax: (310) 247-1111
Also repped by:
The Gold/Miller Company

This rubber-faced comedian became the world's most highly paid actor for a brief period when Sony Pictures' Mark Canton riled competitors by offering him $20 million to star in the dark comedy *Cable Guy*. Despite that film's fuzzy reception, Carrey has proven himself to be one of the industry's most bankable stars—even when he has less than Oscar-caliber material to work with. His $100 million–plus domestic performances in *Ace Ventura: When Nature Calls*, *Dumb and Dumber*, *The Mask*, and *Liar Liar* have made him the first pick for physical comedies. But there's more to Carrey than just shtick, as he proved to Hollywood and the rest of the world with his 1998 role in Peter Weir's critically acclaimed—but Academy-snubbed—*The Truman Show*. He followed *Truman* with the 1999 Andy Kaufman biopic *Man on the Moon*. After making the rounds of comedy clubs and landing the 1991 Showtime special *Jim Carrey's Unnatural Act*, the Canadian funny man caught the public's eye in the early '90s as a member of Fox TV's talented *In Living Color* troupe.

SEAN CONNERY

Fountainbridge Films

With a career that spans an astounding five decades, Connery is still a top box-office draw as he enters the new millennium—and he has an eight-figure per pic salary to show for it. The

SEAN CONNERY (CON'T)

8428 Melrose Pl.
Unit C
Los Angeles, CA 90069
Phone: (323) 782-1177
Fax: (323) 852-9327
Repped by:
Creative Artists Agency

Scottish-born high school dropout, who made his film debut in the 1950s, is still best known for his work as the suave British agent 007, a role he personified in seven James Bond pics. But he reinvented himself as an irascible iconoclast with a heart of gold in the '90s with roles in *The Untouchables*, for which he won a Supporting Actor Oscar, *The Rock*, and *The Hunt for Red October*. While he's known in the industry as a demanding perfectionist—and for making perfection look easy—Connery has had his share of big-budget failures, including *First Knight*, *Rising Sun*, *A Good Man in Africa*, and *Just Cause*. In 1994, he formed Fountainbridge Films with his longtime development exec Rhonda Tollefson. The pair moved their deal from Fox (for which they produced the 1999 Connery-starrer *Entrapment*) to Disney before inking simultaneous agreements with Sony Pictures and indie Intermedia.

KEVIN COSTNER

c/o Harley Williams
Blanc, Williams,
Johnston & Kronstad
1900 Avenue of the Stars
17th Floor
Los Angeles, CA 90067
Phone: (310) 552-2500
Fax: (310) 552-1191

Despite his scenes ending up on the cutting room floor in the 1983 film *The Big Chill*, Costner's All-American good looks and stoic delivery helped him ascend to superstardom rather quickly—maintaining that perch has been a problem, however. Costner built his reputation as one of Hollywood's biggest draws in the mid-to-late '80s, when he starred in such pics as *Silverado*, *No Way Out*, *Bull Durham*, and *Field of Dreams*. Those films put him on the A-list, with the prerequisite eight-figure salary and perks. Costner seemed to enter a new stratosphere with his 1990 directorial debut, *Dances with Wolves*, an epic that became a surprise box office hit and won seven Oscars, including Best Picture and Best Director. Costner's follow-ups included *JFK*, *Robin Hood: Prince of Thieves*, *The Bodyguard*, and *A Perfect World* (one of his best-reviewed but least-seen roles). But beginning with *Wyatt Earp* and *The War* in 1994, Costner's career has been on an extended skid, marked by ill-advised roles in such pics as *Waterworld* (aka *Fishtar* and *Kevin's Gate*), which turned out to be a logistical and press nightmare with a bloated budget and mediocre reviews. While Costner's subsequent roles in such films as *Tin Cup* (1996) and *Message in a Bottle* (1999) have garnered lukewarm responses from audiences, the biggest high-profile failure of his career was *The Postman* (1997), the disastrous three-hour sci-fi epic that marked his sophomore outing as a director. Costner is looking to right his recent woes by returning to the baseball diamond in *For the Love of the Game*, directed by Sam Raimi.

TOM CRUISE

Cruise-Wagner Prods.
c/o Paramount Pictures
5555 Melrose Ave.
Los Angeles, CA 90038
Phone: (323) 956-8150
Fax: (323) 862-1250
Repped by:
Creative Artists Agency

Since he won over audiences as a mischievous high schooler dancing in his BVDs in 1983's *Risky Business*, Cruise has emerged as perhaps the most consistent box-office draw of any Hollywood star. His success is probably due in equal parts to his boyish charm, which appeals to both men and women, and to the care with which he has chosen his roles. Cruise's credits include the \$100 million–plus domestic grossers *Mission: Impossible* (\$181 million), *Top Gun* (\$177 million); *Rain Man* ($173 million), *The Firm* ($158 million), *Jerry Maguire* ($154 million), *A Few Good Men* ($141 million), and *Interview with the Vampire* ($105 million). He was out of circulation for well over a year starting in 1997, while he and his wife, Nicole Kidman, toiled on director Stanley Kubrick's controversial final effort, *Eyes Wide Shut*, before moving on in 1999 to *Mission: Impossible 2*. In 1992, Cruise and his former CAA agent, Paula Wagner, formed Cruise-Wagner Prods. and signed an exclusive deal with Paramount. Three years later, the much sought-after pair renewed their ties with Par, this time negotiating a non-exclusive pact. Unlike many star producing arrangements, which are little more than vanity deals, the partnership has yielded *Mission* and its sequel, as well as the Steve Prefontaine biopic *Without Limits*.

ROBERT DE NIRO

Tribeca Productions
375 Greenwich St.
Eighth Floor
New York, NY 10013
Phone: (212) 941-4000
Fax: (212) 941-4044
Repped by:
Creative Artists Agency

Between producing through Tribeca Films, directing, and acting, Robert De Niro is finding himself stretched to the limit. Though always an actor's actor, De Niro has shifted somewhat in his choices. He took the action film *Ronin*, for example, because he was paid $12 million. While De Niro will never see $20 million against 20 percent of the gross numbers, he can always pound out a decent interpretation of a role, whether he's asking you if you're talking to him or rubbing out some wiseguy. His roles are priceless, with such films as *The Godfather, Part II*; *Taxi Driver*; *Goodfellas*; *Casino*; *Heat*; *Awakenings*; *The King of Comedy*; *Raging Bull*;

and *Midnight Run*. But he's also impeccable in the less stressed roles: *Falling in Love*, *Stanley and Iris*, *Backdraft*, *Cape Fear*, *Jackknife*, *Brazil*, *Mad Dog and Glory*, *Night and the City*, *Marvin's Room*, and *Cop Land*.

CAMERON DIAZ

c/o International Creative Management
8942 Wilshire Blvd.
Beverly Hills, CA 90211
Phone: (310) 550-4000
Fax: (310) 550-4100
Also repped by: Artists Management Group

Like her hair in the Farrelly brothers' gross-out comedy *There's Something About Mary*, Diaz's career has gone straight up in recent years. Which isn't to say that the part-Cuban, part–Native American actress's career hasn't had its share of down moments. In 1989, at the tender age of sixteen, Diaz launched a successful modeling career with the Elite agency. Her first feature, the 1994 Jim Carrey–starrer *The Mask*, was a huge hit, but it was followed by the considerably less successful *The Last Supper*, *Feeling Minnesota*, and *She's the One*. Her next hit was 1997's *My Best Friend's Wedding*, which was followed by less-than-stellar roles in *A Life Less Ordinary*, *Head Above Water*, and the ensemble black comedy *Very Bad Things*. But her role in *Mary*, as the luminously beautiful, fun-loving, yet down-to-earth babe (who at the end of an evening invites her date over to watch *Sports Center*) catapulted her into the elite $10-million-per-pic actress club.

LEONARDO DICAPRIO

As the star of the top-grossing film of all time, Leonardo DiCaprio emerged as the true king of the world, earning a $20 million payday for his follow-up, *The Beach*, directed by *Trainspotting*

LEONARDO DICAPRIO (CON'T)

c/o Artists Management Group
9465 Wilshire Blvd.
Suite 519
Beverly Hills, CA 90212
Phone: (310) 860-8000
Fax: (310) 271-9753

helmer Danny Boyle. Industry watchers note that while *Titanic* put him on top of the global stage, it was Baz Luhrmann's 1996 pic, *William Shakespeare's Romeo + Juliet*, that served as the actor's calling card to the bigtime. While there is speculation his mass teen appeal will wane as his fans age and as he chooses roles less leading-mannish, like *What's Eating Gilbert Grape*, for the early years of the new millennium his place is secure as one of the industry's biggest stars. Not surprisingly, after *Titanic* Hollywood studios began a stampede to get the actor in their movies, and DiCaprio has numerous projects being developed for him around town, including *Gangs of New York,* which would team him with Martin Scorsese, and an untitled Howard Hughes biopic to be helmed by Michael Mann.

MICHAEL DOUGLAS

Furthur Films
c/o Universal Pictures
100 Universal City Plaza
Universal City, CA 91608
Phone: (818) 777-6700
Fax: (818) 866-1278
Repped by:
Creative Artists Agency

Douglas, who has enjoyed more than two decades of success as an actor and producer, inked a multiyear, first-look production deal for his Furthur Films with Universal in December 1997. Douglas got his start as the co-star with Karl Malden of the mid-'70s TV cop show *The Streets of San Francisco* before making his feature producing debut (in collaboration with Saul Zaentz) on the 1975 Milos Forman–helmed Oscar-winner *One Flew over the Cuckoo's Nest*. Douglas's career as a big-screen star didn't start flying until the '80s with such pics as *Romancing the Stone* (1984), its sequel *Jewel of the Nile* (1985), Oliver Stone's *Wall Street* (1987), and

Danny DeVito's *War of the Roses* (1989). To latter-day audiences, Douglas became known for a string of roles where he—some might say fantastically—falls victim to beautiful, sexually predatory women: *Fatal Attraction* (1987), *Basic Instinct* (1992), and *Disclosure* (1994). Other recent roles are in *Falling Down* (1993), *The American President* (1995), *The Ghost and the Darkness* (1996), *The Game* (1997), and *The Perfect Murder* (1998), in which he's paired with the three-decades-younger Gwyneth Paltrow. As a producer, Douglas's Stonebridge Entertainment was involved with Joel Schumacher's *Flatliners* (1990), Richard Donner's *Radio Flyer* (1992), and Richard Benjamin's *Made in America* (1993). In 1994, Douglas teamed with former Regency exec Steve Reuther and German financier Bodo Scriba in Constellation Films, which inked a deal to to co-finance pics with Paramount. Before its German funding dried up, they produced *Sabrina*, *The Ghost and the Darkness*, and *The Rainmaker*. Reuther and Douglas split in 1997, shortly before Douglas formed Furthur.

HARRISON FORD

c/o Patricia McQueeney
McQueeney Management
10279 Century Woods Dr.
Los Angeles, CA 90067
Phone: (310) 277-1882
Fax: (310) 788-0985

Harrison Ford gave up acting when he was twenty-six years old and worked as a carpenter in Hollywood, building an elaborate entrance for Francis Ford Coppola's offices at the Goldwyn Studios. It was three years before he signed up for the low-budget *American Graffiti* (1973), for a young director named George Lucas. Four years later, he was cast as Han Solo in *Star Wars*, and

Ford never looked back, starting a string of A-list, high-profile films like *Raiders of the Lost Ark*, *Indiana Jones and the Temple of Doom*, *Working Girl*, *Presumed Innocent*, *Regarding Henry*, *Patriot Games*, *The Fugitive*, *Clear and Present Danger*, *Sabrina*, *The Devil's Own*, and *Air Force One*. Ford's pricetag is $20 million against 20 percent of the gross, which he should maintain for the time being. His *Six Days, Seven Nights*, opposite Anne Heche, didn't perform in the U.S., but did fine overseas. Now, he's considering a number of films, not the least of which is another Indiana Jones sequel. And he's not producing any of them.

JODIE FOSTER

Egg Productions
c/o Paramount Pictures
5555 Melrose Ave.
Los Angeles, CA 90038
Phone: (323) 956-8400
Fax: (323) 862-1414
Repped by: International Creative Management

Foster has not only survived the often perilous transition from child actor to adult star, she has thrived as a producer and director whose focus and integrity add an aura of prestige to any project with which she's affiliated. Which isn't to say she hasn't had her share of clunkers. Foster got her first national exposure in 1966 at age three, as the Coppertone girl in a TV commercial, before appearing on such sitcoms as *Mayberry R.F.D.* and *The Courtship of Eddie's Father*. But it was her role as a pre-teen hooker in Martin Scorsese's 1976 classic *Taxi Driver* that garnered her first public attention—not to mention an Oscar nomination. After attending Yale, she won her first Oscar for the role of rape victim in *The Accused* (1988). Three years later she got a second statuette for her role as a rookie FBI agent opposite Anthony Hopkins in *The Silence of the Lambs*. That same year she made her feature directorial debut on 1991's *Little Man Tate*, in which she also starred. Her next big box office role was as a sexy con artist in the 1994 Mel Gibson–starrer *Maverick*, one of her few comedies. She returned to serious fare as an alien-hunting scientist in *Contact* (1997).

In 1992, Foster formed her Egg Productions banner, inking a rich three-year production deal with now defunct PolyGram Filmed Entertainment, effectively giving her greenlight power on several mid-budgeted pics, including the 1994 pic *Nell*, directed by Michael Apted. The deal also produced Foster's second directorial effort, the slight ensemble comedy *Home for the Holidays* (1995). After PolyGram was bought out by Seagram, Foster moved her Egg logo over to Paramount, where she inked a deal to produce, direct, and star in features for the studio.

MEL GIBSON

Icon Productions
c/o Paramount Pictures
5555 Melrose Ave.
Wilder Building
Los Angeles, CA 90038
Phone: (323) 956-2100
Fax: (323) 862-2121
Repped by: International Creative Management

As one of the industry's top-paid actors, Gibson reportedly broke the $20 million upfront fee barrier on *Lethal Weapon 4*, for which he also commanded a healthy chunk of the gross. His deal on Sony's Revolutionary War pic (working title *The Patriot*) is believed to be one of the richest ever for a thesp. But Gibson, who has been a producer, knows what it's like to sit on the other side of the desk. Born in the U.S., he moved to Australia at age twelve. After doing Shakespeare in a Sydney theater company, he made his feature debut in George Miller's 1979 release *Mad Max*, followed by Peter Weir's *Gallipoli* (1981), made in Australia as *Mad Max 2* Miller's *The Road Warrior* (1981), and Weir's *The Year of Living Danger-*

ously (1983). While his 1984 American film debut, *The River,* didn't make much of a splash, Gibson rocketed to superstar status as borderline crazy cop Martin Riggs in 1987's *Lethal Weapon*, a film followed by three lucrative sequels over the next 11 years. In 1990, Gibson and producing partner Bruce Davy's Icon Prods. made its producing debut on the Franco Zeffirelli–helmed *Hamlet*, in which Gibson played the haunted Danish prince. Gibson took his first turn in the director's chair with the 1993 flop *The Man Without a Face*. His second helming effort, *Braveheart*, was considerably more successful, pairing box-office lucre with Oscar gold. Gibson turned in solid performances in *Ransom* (1996), *Conspiracy Theory* (1997), *Lethal Weapon 4* (1998), and *Payback* (1999). Evidence, if any is needed, of Gibson's power: Unhappy with his character in *Payback*, he demanded—and got—re-shoots, against the wishes of first-time director Brian Helgeland.

TOM HANKS

The Playtone Company
P.O. Box 7340
Santa Monica, CA 90406
Phone: (310) 394-5700
Fax: (310) 394-4466
Repped by:
Creative Artists Agency

Does anyone morph quite as successfully as Tom Hanks does into different roles? He has shifted from an AIDS patient in *Philadelphia* to a man-child in *Forrest Gump* to a war-weary sergeant in *Saving Private Ryan*. Hanks has been rewarded for his efforts with back-to-back Oscars for Best Actor. He also earns an obscene amount of cash on these projects. On *Ryan*, he wasn't paid much upfront, but he and Spielberg took in a total of 50 percent of the gross. He's producing a slew of projects with partner Gary Goetzman, including the HBO miniseries *Band of Brothers* and the thirteen-parter *From the Earth to the Moon*. Upcoming for Hanks will be *Toy Story 2*, *Where the Wild Things Are*, *Gump & Co*. (the sequel), *The Power Broker* (based on the Robert Caro bio of Robert Moses), an untitled project for Martin Scorsese about Walter Winchell, and *The Passion of Richard Nixon*, where he'll play the president. But first will be *Cast Away*, opposite Helen Hunt.

DUSTIN HOFFMAN

Punch Productions
11661 San Vicente Blvd.
Suite 222
Los Angeles, CA 90049
Phone: (310) 442-4880
Fax: (310) 442-4884
Repped by: International Creative Management

Dustin Hoffman can still demand acting work, though he no longer will be making as much dough as the new generation of top earners. Lately, he's knocked out some smaller showcases like *Wag the Dog*, along with some out-of-place action work like *Sphere*, both for director Barry Levinson. But he will always have *The Graduate*, *Midnight Cowboy*, *Lenny*, *All the President's Men*, *Kramer vs. Kramer*, *Tootsie*, *Rain Man*, and *Little Big Man* to fall back on. His lukewarm approaches to action include *Outbreak*, which he took after it had been turned down by Harrison Ford. For Hoffman now, the move is producing with his new label, Punch Productions. He's already got *A Walk on the Moon* earning raves, and *Viola d'Amore*, *The House of Mirth*, *The Furies*, *Life and Death on 10 West*, and *Golden Rule* in development.

HELEN HUNT

Hunt/Tavel Productions

She's not exactly the new girl on the block, with more than twenty-six years in show business, but Helen Hunt has finally jumped to the

HELEN HUNT (CON'T)

10202 West Washington Blvd.
Astaire Bldg.
Room 2410
Culver City, CA 90232
Phone: (310) 244-3144
Fax: (310) 244-0164
Repped by:
Creative Artists Agency

upper echelons of female stardom in Hollywood. The Oscar she earned for *As Good As It Gets* often has that effect. She suddenly went from starring on the TV show *Mad About You* to toplining major feature films. Her credits had not been that impressive—*Project X*, *Next of Kin*, *The Waterdance*, *Mr. Saturday Night*, *Kiss of Death*, and *Twister*—but her next step, in *Cast Away* opposite Tom Hanks for Bob Zemeckis, will be upwardly mobile. With her newly created production deal at Sony Pictures Entertainment, Hunt is slowly moving into production and directing, with *Then She Found Me*, *She's Funny That Way*, *Round Rock*, *Mama Masai*, and *Count the Raindrops* in development.

TOMMY LEE JONES

c/o International Creative Management
8942 Wilshire Blvd.
Beverly Hills, CA 90211
Phone: (310) 550-4000
Fax: (310) 550-4100

After over two decades as an underrated supporting player, Jones's Oscar-winning performance in Andrew Davis's *The Fugitive* won him a new generation of fans—and an eight-digit salary. The Texas-born Harvard grad made his feature debut with a small role in the 1970 tearjerker *Love Story*, before spending four years on TV as Dr. Mark Toland in the ABC soap *One Life to Live*. He continued with stage work before getting his first leading feature role in *Jackson County Jail* (1976), which he followed with roles in the 1978 megaflop *The Betsy*, *The Eyes of Laura Mars* (1978), and *Coal Miner's Daughter* (1980). After a brief lull, during which Jones appeared mainly in cable pics, he was perfectly cast as the stoic Texas Ranger Woodrow

Call in the CBS miniseries *Lonesome Dove* (1988). Later film roles were in Mike Figgis's *Stormy Monday* (1988), Davis's *The Package* (1989), Oliver Stone's *JFK* (1991) (for which he was nominated for Best Supporting Actor Oscar), *Under Siege* (1992), and *The Fugitive* (1993). His taut portrayal of a wily U.S. marshal—and the critical and public response to it—led to *Blown Away*, *The Client*, *Natural Born Killers*, and *Cobb* (all 1994); *Batman Forever* (1995); *Volcano* and *Men in Black* (both 1997); and the uninspired *Fugitive* sequel, *U.S. Marshals* (1998).

EDDIE MURPHY

c/o William Morris Agency
151 El Camino Dr.
Beverly Hills, CA 90212
Phone: (310) 859-4000
Fax: (310) 859-4462

Eddie Murphy will always be able to open a film. The question is, can he sustain it? Murphy's *Life* opened to $20.7 million in April 1999 but then it dropped off significantly. He has had his share of winners lately with *Dr. Dolittle* and *The Nutty Professor*, both of which are being readied for sequels. But after turning thirty-eight in 1999, Murphy needs other adult roles. His ventures into action (*Metro*) haven't worked; but his credits are still stellar, with *Beverly Hills Cop*, *Distinguished Gentleman*, *48 HRS*, *Trading Places*, and *Coming to America* topping the list. But he needs to find transition roles that will allow him to flow into the millennium. He's castable enough, but the roles have to mean something. "So what if my career dies?" he told the *Daily News*. "I stopped thinking in terms of career $80 million ago. If it ends, I'll sit home and chill and raise babies."

JACK NICHOLSON

c/o Sandy Bresler
Bresler-Kelly & Associates
11550 West Olympic Blvd.
Suite 510
Los Angeles, CA 90064
Phone: (310) 479-5611
Fax: (310) 479-3775

Jack Nicholson will always be Jack. And as long as he can churn out performances like his Oscar winner in *As Good As It Gets* or the "You can't handle the truth" Colonel in *A Few Good Men*, he will always be one of Hollywood's top money earners. He has been through several careers as an actor, starting with the B-movies that he toplined for nearly a decade, then the early '70s films like *The Last Detail*, *The King of Marvin Gardens*, *Chinatown*, *Carnal Knowledge*, and *One Flew over the Cuckoo's Nest.* He later segued into all sorts of films, from *Prizzi's Honor* to *Reds* to *Terms of Endearment*. In 1989, he starred in *Batman* with a deal so rich in merchandising rights, he made money on the sequel, *Batman Returns*, without even acting in it. He's always a regular at the Laker games and he's a loyal friend. His name is up for a number of new roles, but he may be most interested in *The Murder of Napoleon* because he'll likely direct the indie film.

GWYNETH PALTROW

c/o Creative Artists Agency
9830 Wilshire Blvd.
Beverly Hills, CA 90212
Phone: (310) 288-4545
Fax: (310) 288-4800

Before her Oscar-winning performance as the Bard's muse in *Shakespeare in Love*, Paltrow had graced the covers of oodles of fashion magazines, but made little impact on the box office. Her previous highest-grossing pics were *Se7en* (1997), in which she had a relatively small part opposite onetime boyfriend Brad Pitt; *A Perfect Murder* (1998), opposite a more-than-twice-her-age Michael Douglas; and *Sliding Doors* (1998), which fared considerably better overseas than in the U.S. Other outings included the art-house hit

Emma, and box-office flops *Jefferson in Paris*, *Moonlight and Valentino*, *Hard Eight*, *Great Expectations*, *The Pallbearer*, and *Mrs. Parker and the Vicious Circle*. As the daughter of actress Blythe Danner and TV producer Bruce Paltrow, she is Hollywood aristocracy. The willowy actress got her first break when family friend Steven Spielberg cast her as the young Wendy in the 1991 pic *Hook*. In 1999, Paltrow starred opposite Matt Damon in Anthony Minghella's *The Talented Mr. Ripley* and *Duets*, directed by her father, with Scott Speedman in the role that at one point had been earmarked for Pitt.

BRAD PITT

c/o Creative Artists Agency
9830 Wilshire Blvd.
Beverly Hills, CA 90212
Phone: (310) 288-4545
Fax: (310) 288-4800
Also repped by:
Brillstein-Grey Entertainment

In a Cinderella-like tale, Brad Pitt emerged from guest spots on such TV series as *Dallas* in the late '80s to become one of the highest-paid leading men of the '90s. After leaping into the spotlight in 1991 with his role as a hitchhiker/thief who seduces Geena Davis in *Thelma & Louise*, Pitt never looked back, racking up a list of credits that include *Johnny Suede*, *Cool World*, and *A River Runs Through It* in 1992; *Kalifornia* and *True Romance* in 1993; *Legends of the Fall* and *Interview with the Vampire* in 1994; and in 1995, *Se7en* and *Twelve Monkeys*, an outing that earned him a Best Supporting Actor Oscar nomination. Audiences stayed home, however, for his high-profile roles in *Sleepers* (1996) and his teaming with Harrison Ford in the 1997 pic *The Devil's Own*, for which Pitt was paid $10 million. He earned that same amount for *Seven Years in Tibet* (1997), a payday that was soon eclipsed by the reported $17.5 million Pitt earned for Universal Pictures' *Meet Joe Black* (1998). While he has had several missteps in recent years and is in need of a hit, Pitt remains a huge draw overseas and seems to have taken a more active role in selecting films based on material rather than being part of a high-profile "package."

KEANU REEVES

c/o Creative Artists Agency
9830 Wilshire Blvd.
Beverly Hills, CA 90212
Phone: (310) 288-4545
Fax: (310) 288-4800
Also repped by:
3 Arts Entertainment

With Warner Bros.' sci-fi hit *The Matrix*, Keanu Reeves was back among Hollywood's A-list. Reeves, who first showed himself to be a bankable leading man with *Speed*, has made more right moves than wrong, and his salary reflects this good fortune. He sidestepped the *Speed 2* debacle for *The Devil's Advocate*, then moved to big success in *The Matrix*, one of 1999's top-grossing films. Reeves is expected to receive a career-best $15 million against a healthy back-end gross for *Shooter*, the Paramount film based on *Point of Impact*, a novel by Stephen Hunter. *Shooter* is being targeted for a start date late in 1999, after Reeves finishes starring for director Howard Deutch in the Warner Bros. gridiron film *The Replacements*, for which he got paid $12.5 million against 12.5 percent of the gross.

JULIA ROBERTS

With her role in Universal Pictures' upcoming *Erin Brockovich*, Julia Roberts became the highest-paid female actress in history, earning a

JULIA ROBERTS (CON'T)

c/o International Creative Management
8942 Wilshire Blvd.
Beverly Hills, CA 90211
Phone: (310) 550-4000
Fax: (310) 550-4100

reported $20 million (her previous high was $17.5 million for *Runaway Bride*). Though that twinkly-eyed innocence that helped launch her into stardom seems to have faded with the years of media and public scrutiny, Roberts maintains her position as one of the industry's most popular stars. With nearly $2 billion in worldwide box office receipts behind her, she cemented her status as the most bankable female star with such pics as *Pretty Woman*, *My Best Friend's Wedding*, *The Pelican Brief*, and *Sleeping with the Enemy*, all of which grossed more than $100 million domestically. Though she has been nominated twice—for Best Supporting Actress in 1989 for her role in *Steel Magnolias* and, a year later, for Best Actress for her turn in *Pretty Woman*—an Oscar win has eluded her. Roberts showed that she was not invincible with such critical and box office also-rans as *I Love Trouble*, *Ready to Wear*, and *Mary Reilly*. She has found a home in recent years as the distaff side in romantic pairings with Mel Gibson in *Conspiracy Theory*, with Hugh Grant in *Notting Hill*, and with Richard Gere in *Runaway Bride*.

MEG RYAN

Prufrock Pictures
335 North Maple Dr.
Suite 135
Beverly Hills, CA 90210
Phone: (310) 285-2360
Fax: (310) 888-3595

Meg Ryan has advanced to the A-list of female actors in Hollywood. She can pick the roles she wants and expect them all to show a decent box office, such as *You've Got Mail*, which she did with Tom Hanks to more than $100 million domestic. And she can always be depended on for perky roles in such films as *When Harry Met Sally . . .*, *Prelude to a Kiss*, *Sleepless in Seattle*,

MEG RYAN (CON'T)

Repped by: International Creative Management

Joe Versus the Volcano, and *City of Angels*. Ryan, however, will also surprise audiences with a downward turn: an alcoholic mother in *When a Man Loves a Woman*, a trussed-up go-go dancer in *Hurlyburly*, or a U.S. Army captain in the Gulf War in *Courage Under Fire*. With T. S. Eliot's "The Love Song of J. Alfred Prufrock" as the namesake basis for her Prufrock Productions banner, it's no surprise that her dream role is to play poet Sylvia Plath. In the meantime, she's attached to produce and possibly star in *When I Close My Eyes* and to co-star with Julia Roberts in *The Women* for New Line Cinema.

ADAM SANDLER

c/o Endeavor Agency
9701 Wilshire Blvd.
Beverly Hills, CA 90212
Phone: (310) 248-2000
Fax: (310) 248-2020
Also repped by: Brillstein-Grey Entertainment

Sandler went from *Saturday Night Live* cast member to top-grossing, eight-figure payday superstar in just a few short years. After his portrayal of Opera Man earned him a regular spot on *SNL,* he landed his first feature starring role in the 1995 comedy *Billy Madison*, which he also co-wrote with former NYU roommate Tim Herlihy. That same year, Sandler's comedy song "The Hanukkah Song" was in heavy rotation on radio playlists. He reteamed with Herlihy to write the Dennis Dugan–helmed golf comedy *Happy Gilmore* (1996), and starred the following year opposite Damon Wayans in the action-comedy *Bulletproof.* While his earlier *Caddyshack*-inspired slapstick pics appealed to a limited audience of young guys, it was with the 1998 romantic comedy *The Wedding Singer* that Sandler crossed over to more mainstream auds. Later that year, the blockbuster sports comedy

The Waterboy (directed by Sandler's NYU buddy Frank Coraci) pushed him even further into the mainstream. In summer 1999, he starred in the Dugan-helmed comedy *Big Daddy*.

ARNOLD SCHWARZENEGGER

c/o William Morris Agency
151 El Camino Dr.
Beverly Hills, CA 90212
Phone: (310) 859-4000
Fax: (310) 859-4462
Repped by:
William Morris Agency

Ah-nuld has been out of sight for a couple of years, waiting to find the right role. He may have found it in *End of Days* for Beacon Pictures. But the general fear around the Schwarzenegger household is that his leading man days are past, largely because the action hero isn't the same as he once was in Hollywood. Roles that Schwarzenegger or Stallone or even Harrison Ford might gravitate toward are few and far between. Still one of Hollywood's highest-paid actors in the $20 million/20 percent of the gross club, Schwarzenegger will always bring box office to the table. He made even more than that for his twenty-minute role as Mr. Freeze in *Batman and Robin*. His relationship with Jim Cameron has always been phenomenal, with *Terminator*, *Terminator 2: Judgment Day*, and *True Lies* to show for it. So it makes complete sense that he's in line for another sequel for his "I'll be back . . . " ubermensch. At the same time, he wants to continue doing comedies and lighter fare, and maybe more directing.

WILL SMITH

Overbrook Entertainment

The hottest new actor to join the $20 million/20 percent of the gross club, Will Smith seems invincible. His roles in *Bad Boys*, *Independence*

WILL SMITH (CON'T)
100 Universal City Plaza
Building 489
Universal City, CA 91608
Phone: (818) 777-2224
Fax: (818) 866-5440
Repped by:
Creative Artists Agency

Day, *Men in Black*, *Enemy of the State*, and *Wild Wild West* have bumped him to the top of the list of young, eligible male leads. He also raps, which is a plus for his agents and managers, considering his lucrative soundtrack opportunities. His new production company, Overbrook Entertainment (named after his high school in Philadelphia), is setting up film projects at various studios, including *A Star Is Born* for Warner Bros. His next role, however, will definitely be *Muhammad Ali* for Columbia Pictures and director Barry Sonnenfeld. And at some point, he and Martin Lawrence are committed to *Bad Boys 2*, also for Columbia.

SYLVESTER STALLONE

c/o William Morris Agency
151 El Camino Dr.
Beverly Hills, CA 90212
Phone: (310) 859-4000
Fax: (310) 859-4462
Also repped by Brillstein-Grey Entertainment

Criticized for being a one-trick action pony, in 1997 (following the tepid response domestically to his 1996 actioner, *Daylight*), former box-office hero Sylvester Stallone took on James Mangold's *Cop Land*, a film intended to showcase the *Rambo* and *Rocky* star's range and acting ability. While he did receive mostly positive notices for his role as a small-town cop, the offers for serious roles didn't come flooding forth, and Stallone failed to take advantage of any heat the film generated. During that time, Stallone wasn't sedentary, however—he managed to change agencies three times in the two years between *Cop Land* and his next starring role, in Universal's *Detox*. (During that span he lent his voice to DreamWorks' *Antz* and made a cameo in the awful pic *Burn, Hollywood, Burn*). *Detox*, which began production in early 1999, is not part of the $60 million, three-picture deal Stallone signed with Universal in 1995. Because his drawing power is now a question mark, the studio restructured that original deal and Stallone's payday for *Detox* is closer to the $17.5 million he was paid for *Daylight* in 1996. Universal is, however, counting on Stallone's still-strong popularity overseas, where he generally brings in twice as much in gross receipts as he does stateside.

JOHN TRAVOLTA

c/o William Morris Agency
151 El Camino Dr.
Beverly Hills, CA 90212
Phone: (310) 859-4000
Fax: (310) 859-4462

John Travolta has churned out more than two films a year for the past five years, following his career resurrection after *Pulp Fiction* hit in 1994. He had *Get Shorty*, *White Man's Burden*, *Broken Arrow*, *Phenomenon*, Nora Ephron's *Michael*, John Woo's *Face/Off*, Costa-Gavras's *Mad City*, Mike Nichols's *Primary Colors*, and Steve Zaillian's *A Civil Action*, the last two of which each garnered him $20 million, as well as a small role in Terence Malick's *The Thin Red Line* and an indie film from Nick Cassavetes, *She's So Lovely*. Travolta is not always the easiest to work with. He walked off the set of *The Double* for Roman Polanski in 1997, an act almost ignored by the media. Though he's an avowed Scientologist, he keeps the church separate from his reel life, for the most part. Next up for him are *Battlefield Earth*, based on Scientology founder L. Ron Hubbard's sci-fi novel, and *Standing Room Only*, the Jimmy Roselli story about the anti-mob lounge act.

DENZEL WASHINGTON

Mundy Lane Entertainment
c/o 20th Century Fox
10201 West Pico Blvd.
Building 31
Los Angeles, CA 90035
Phone: (310) 369-5940
Fax: (310) 369-8330
Repped by: International Creative Management

Though Denzel Washington's recent films (*Fallen*, *He Got Game*, *The Siege*) have faltered at the box office, he continues to be one of the highest-paid and hardest-working actors in the business today. The $12-million-a-picture star has strung together several starring roles for 1999 and 2000, including a quadriplegic detective in *The Bone Collector*, directed by Phillip Noyce, and the title role of former middleweight champ Rubin "Hurricane" Carter in *Lazarus and the Hurricane*, a Norman Jewison–directed biopic about the fighter who was twice wrongfully imprisoned for the murder of three whites in a New Jersey bar. Washington is expected to make his directorial debut on Fox Searchlight's *Finding Fish*, an autobiographical rags-to-riches tale of Antwone Fisher, a former security guard on the Sony Pictures lot who turned his life story into a script. Though Washington, who won an Oscar for *Glory*, is one of the most respected thesps in Hollywood, his films have trouble breaking out, unless he is teamed with another star of equal caliber (like Tom Hanks in *Philadelphia*, Gene Hackman in *Crimson Tide*, or Julia Roberts in *Pelican Brief*).

ROBIN WILLIAMS

Blue Wolf Productions
725 Arizona Ave.
Suite 202
Santa Monica, CA 90401

Robin Williams stirred up more heat for defecting from Creative Artists Agency and going to Mike Ovitz's Artists Management Group than he has for any of his movies of late. His most recent hit was *Patch Adams*, which was roundly denounced by the critics, but loved by the paying audiences. His career has had its hits-and-misses

ROBIN WILLIAMS (CON'T)

Phone: (310) 451-8890
Fax: (310) 451-4886
Repped by:
Artists Management Group

with *Good Will Hunting*, *Flubber*, and *The Birdcage* earning their keep, while *What Dreams May Come*, *Father's Day*, and *Jack* have tanked. But he keeps plugging along, with his wife and producer, Marsha Williams, helping his cause. His overall credits are too good to overlook, with roles in *Mrs. Doubtfire*; *Toys*; *The Fisher King*; *Hook*; *Dead Again*; *Cadillac Man*; *Awakenings*; *Dead Poets Society*; *The Adventures of Baron Munchausen*; *Good Morning, Vietnam*; *Moscow on the Hudson*; *The World According to Garp*; and *Popeye*. But most agree that he has yet to live up to his full potential. Next up was *Jakob the Liar*, which is about a man who protects his child from the Nazis, and then the big-budget sci-fi domestic yarn *The Bicentennial Man*, for Disney and Sony.

BRUCE WILLIS

Flying Heart Films
11301 West Olympic Blvd.
Los Angeles, CA 90064
Phone: (310) 360-9464
Fax: (310) 854-4996
Repped by:
William Morris Agency

Bruce Willis could hold claim to the title of hardest-working man in showbiz, having appeared in nearly thirty films since his starmaking ABC TV series *Moonlighting* went off the air in 1989. During those years (and not including the three films he shot during the series, among them the first *Die Hard*), the New Jersey native has starred in his share of bombs (*Hudson Hawk*, *Bonfire of the Vanities*, and *Color of Night*, to name a few). But he's also managed to put together a list of credits that include box office blockbusters such as *Die Hard* and its sequels *Die Hard 2* (1990) and *Die Hard with a Vengeance* (1995), and critically lauded turns in such pics as *In Country* (1989), *Nobody's Fool*

(1994), *Pulp Fiction* (1994), and *Twelve Monkeys* (1995). While Willis seemed to sleepwalk through outings like *Last Man Standing*, *The Jackal*, and *Mercury Rising*, he showed that he still commands attention as a smirky action star in *The Fifth Element* and *Armageddon*. In recent years, Willis has been turning double duty as producer as well as star on such pics as the indie *Breakfast of Champions* and the upcoming heist caper *Ace*.

ATTORNEYS

ATTORNEYS

These are legal eagles who soar above some of the biggest names and biggest deals in Hollywood.

JAKE BLOOM

Bloom, Hergott, Cook, Diemer & Klein
150 South Rodeo Dr. Third Floor
Beverly Hills, CA 90212
Phone: (310) 859-6880
Fax: (310) 859-2788

Clients include producers Brian Grazer and Jerry Bruckheimer, and thesps Jackie Chan and Nicolas Cage.

HARRY "SKIP" BRITTENHAM

Ziffren, Brittenham, Branca & Fischer
1801 Century Park West
Los Angeles, CA 90067
Phone: (310) 552-3388
Fax: (310) 553-7068

Clients include thesps Harrison Ford, Eddie Murphy, and Bill Murray.

MELANIE COOK

Bloom, Bergott, Book, Diemer & Klein
150 South Rodeo Dr. Third Floor
Beverly Hills, CA 90212
Phone: (310) 859-6890
Fax: (310) 859-2788

Clients include producer Scott Rudin and directors Martin Scorsese, Barry Sonnenfield, and Tim Burton.

CRAIG EMANUEL

Loeb & Loeb LLP
10100 Santa Monica Blvd. Suite 2200
Los Angeles, CA 90067-4164
Phone: (310) 282-2262
Fax: (310) 282-2192

Clients include directors Robert Rodriguez, Alex Proyas, and Iain Softley, and thesp Steven Seagal.

TOM HANSEN AND CRAIG JACOBSON

Hansen, Jacobson, Teller & Hoberman
450 North Roxbury Dr. Eighth Floor
Beverly Hills, CA 90210-4222
Phone: (310) 271-8777
Fax: (310) 276-8310

Clients include Leonardo DiCaprio, Drew Barrymore, Charlize Theron, Meg Ryan, Mel Gibson, and John Woo.

RICHARD HELLER
Frankfurt, Garbus, Klein & Selz
488 Madison Ave. Ninth Floor
New York, NY 10022
Phone: (212) 980-0120
Fax: (212) 593-9175

Clients include writers Tom Clancy and Dean Koontz.

ALAN HERGOTT
Bloom, Hergott, Cook, Diemer & Klein
150 South Rodeo Dr. Third Floor
Beverly Hills, CA 90212
Phone: (310) 859-6803
Fax: (310) 859-2788

Clients include actors Tom Hanks and Russell Crowe.

BARRY HIRSCH
Armstrong, Hirsch, Jackoway,
Tyerman & Wertheimer
1888 Century Park East 18th Floor
Los Angeles, CA 90067
Phone: (310) 553-0305
Fax: (310) 553-5036

Clients include manager/producer Brad Grey and directors Peter Hyams, Simon West, and Francis Ford Coppola.

DEBORAH KLEIN
Bloom, Hergott, Cook, Diemer & Klein
150 South Rodeo Dr. Third Floor
Beverly Hills, CA 90212
Phone: (310) 859-6897
Fax: (310) 859-2788

Clients include managers Rick Yorn and Julie Silverman Yorn, and thesps Jim Carrey and Samuel L. Jackson.

BRUCE RAMER
Gang, Tyrer, Ramer & Brown
132 South Rodeo Dr.
Beverly Hills, CA 90212
Phone: (310) 777-4800
Fax: (310) 777-4801

Clients include directors Tom Shadyac, Clint Eastwood, Steven Spielberg, and Robert Zemeckis, and thesp George Clooney.

IRA SCHRECK
Schreck, Rose & Dapello
660 Madison Ave. 10th Floor
New York, NY 10021
Phone: (212) 826-0360
Fax: (212) 832-2960

Clients include directors Jim Sheridan, Ang Lee, Nicholas Hytner, and Jesse Peretz, and thesps Stephen Baldwin, Natalie Portman, Ed Harris, and Kyra Sedgwick.

JOHN SLOSS
Sloss Law Office
170 Fifth Ave. Suite 800
New York, NY 10010
Phone: (212) 627-9898
Fax: (212) 627-9498

Clients include directors Kevin Smith, Richard Linklater, and Todd Haynes.

Alan Wertheimer

Armstrong, Hirsch, Jackoway,
Tyerman & Wertheimer
1888 Century Park East 18th Floor
Los Angeles, CA 90067
Phone: (310) 553-0305
Fax: (310) 553-5036

Recently negotiated, on behalf of thirty-one top writers (including client Ron Bass), the groundbreaking deal with Sony that gave the scribes, and potentially many more, 2 percent of the gross from films on which they are involved.

ORGANIZATIONS/ ASSOCIATIONS AND GUILDS/UNIONS

ORGANIZATIONS/ASSOCIATIONS AND GUILDS/UNIONS

The following is a list of the leading professional guilds, unions, and associations in the feature film industry.

ORGANIZATIONS/ ASSOCIATIONS

Academy of Motion Picture Arts and Sciences (AMPAS)
8949 Wilshire Blvd.
Beverly Hills, CA 90211-1972
Phone: (310) 247-3000
Fax: (310) 859-9351
Web site: www.oscars.org

Academy of Television Arts & Sciences
5220 Lankershim Blvd.
North Hollywood, CA 91601
Phone: (818) 754-2800
Fax: (818) 761-2827
Web site: www.emmys.org

The Actors Fund of America
4727 Wilshire Blvd. Suite 310
Los Angeles, CA 90010
Phone: (323) 933-9244
Fax: (323) 933-7615

1501 Broadway Suite 518
New York, NY 10036-5697
Phone: (212) 221-7300
Fax: (212) 754-0238

Alliance of Motion Picture & Television Producers
15503 Ventura Blvd.
Encino, CA 91436
Phone: (818) 995-3600
Fax: (818) 382-1793

American Film Institute (AFI)
2021 North Western Ave.
Los Angeles, CA 90027
Phone: (213) 856-7600
Fax: (213) 467-4578
Web site: www.afionline.org

American Film Marketing Association
10850 Wilshire Blvd. Ninth Floor
Los Angeles, CA 90024
Phone: (310) 446-1000
Fax: (310) 446-1600
Web site: www.afma.com/
Trade association

ASCAP (American Society of Composers, Authors and Publishers)

7920 Sunset Blvd. Third Floor
Los Angeles, CA 90046
Phone: (323) 883-1000
Fax: (323) 883-1049
Web site: www.ascap.com/

1 Lincoln Plaza
New York, NY 10023
Phone: (212) 621-6000
Fax: (212) 724-9064

American Women in Radio and Television (AWRT)

1650 Tysons Blvd. Suite 200
McLean, VA 22101
Phone: (703) 506-3290
Fax: (703) 506-3266
Web site: www.awrt.org

Association of Film Commissioners International (AFCI)

7060 Hollywood Blvd.
Los Angeles, CA 90028
Phone: (323) 462-6092
Fax: (323) 462-6091
Web site: www.afciweb.org

Association of Talent Agencies

9255 Sunset Blvd. Suite 930
Los Angeles, CA 90069
Phone: (310) 274-0628
Fax: (310) 274-5063

BMI (Broadcast Music Inc.)

8730 Sunset Blvd. Third Floor West
Los Angeles, CA 90069
Phone: (310) 659-9109
Fax: (310) 657-6947
Web site: www.bmi.com

320 West 57th St.
New York, NY 10019
Phone: (212) 586-2000
Fax: (212) 489-2368

California Arts Council

1300 First St. Suite 930
Sacramento, CA 95814
Phone: (916) 322-6555
Fax: (916) 322-6575
Web site: www.cac.ca.gov/

Casting Society of America

606 North Larchmont Blvd. Suite 4B
Los Angeles, CA 90004
Phone: (323) 463-1925
Fax: (323) 463-5753
Web site: www.castingsociety.com

Independent Feature Project (IFP)

1964 Westwood Blvd. Suite 205
Los Angeles, CA 90025
Phone: (310) 475-4379
Fax: (310) 441-5676
Web site: www.ifpwest.org

Motion Picture and Television Fund

23388 Mulholland Dr.
Woodland Hills, CA 91364
Phone: (818) 876-1888
Fax: (818) 876-1079

Motion Picture Association of America (MPAA)

15503 Ventura Blvd.
Encino, CA 91436
Phone: (818) 995-3600
Web site: www.mpaa.org/

National Academy of Recording Arts and Sciences

3402 Pico Blvd.
Santa Monica, CA 90405
Phone: (310) 392-3777
Fax: (310) 392-2306

National Association of Television Program Executives (NATPE)

2425 Olympic Blvd. Suite 550E
Santa Monica, CA 90404
Phone: (310) 453-4440
Fax: (310) 453-5258
Web site: www.natpe.org

The Organization of Black Screenwriters

P.O. Box 70160
Los Angeles, CA 90070-0160
Phone: (323) 882-4166
Web site: www.OBSwriter.com

Recording Musicians Association (RMA)

817 Vine St. Suite 209
Hollywood, CA 90038
Phone: (323) 462-4762
Fax: (323) 462-2406

Society of Composers and Lyricists

400 South Beverly Dr. Suite 214
Beverly Hills, CA 90212
Phone: (310) 281-2812
Fax: (310) 990-0601
Web site: www.filmscore.org

Women in Film

6464 Sunset Blvd. Suite 1080
Los Angeles, CA 90028
Phone: (323) 463-6040
Fax: (323) 463-0963
Web site: www.wif.org

GUILDS/UNIONS

Actors Equity Association

5757 Wilshire Blvd. Suite 1
Los Angeles, CA 90036
Phone: (323) 869-8530
Fax: (323) 634-1777

165 West 46th St.
New York, NY 10036
Phone: (212) 869-8530
Fax: (212) 719-9815

American Federation of Television and Radio Artists (AFTRA)

5757 Wilshire Blvd. Suite 900
Los Angeles, CA 90036
Phone: (323) 634-8100
Fax: (323) 634-8246

260 Madison Ave. Seventh Floor
New York, NY 10016
Phone: (212) 532-0800
Fax: (212) 545-1238

Director's Guild of America (DGA)

7920 Sunset Blvd.
Los Angeles, CA 90046
Phone: (310) 289-2000
Fax: (310) 289-2029
Agency listing: (213) 851-3671
Web site: www.dga.org/

110 West 57th St.
New York, NY 10019
Phone: (212) 581-0370
Fax: (212) 581-1441

Producers Guild of America (PGA)

400 South Beverly Dr. Suite 211
Beverly Hills, CA 90212
Phone: (310) 557-0807
Fax: (310) 557-0436

Screen Actors Guild (SAG)

5757 Wilshire Blvd.
Los Angeles, CA 90036-3600
Phone: (323) 954-1600
Fax: (323) 954-6603
New membership: (323) 549-6769
Membership services: (323) 549-6778

1515 Broadway 44th Floor
New York, NY 10036
Phone: (212) 944-1030
Fax: (212) 944-6774

Writer's Guild of America, East (WGAE)

555 West 57 St. Suite 1230
New York, NY 10019
Phone: (212) 767-7800
Fax: (212) 582-1909
Web site: www.wgaeast.org

Writer's Guild of America, West (WGAW)

7000 West Third St.
Los Angeles, CA 90048
Phone: (323) 951-4000
Fax: (323) 782-4800
Agency listing: (323) 782-4502
Web site: www.wga.org

TOP GROSSERS, 1996–98

TOP GROSSERS, 1996–98

The following are the top five films for each year from 1996 to 1998. While Hollywood has yet to develop a formula for box office success (after all, "nobody knows anything"), after a quick study of these listings, a composite profile can be constructed. So future studio moguls take note: An almost surefire blockbuster is a PG-13 sci-fi adventure that runs 129 minutes, costs $92.5 million to make, and is released in May or July to make its way to a $510 million worldwide box-office gross. And as far as casting, try Bruce Willis or Will Smith as the hero, with Jean Reno or Jeff Goldblum as a sidekick and Gary Oldman as the baddie. In other words, do everything almost exactly opposite of James Cameron's all-time box office champ *Titanic,* a historical romantic drama that clocked in at over three hours, cost an estimated $220 million to make, was released in December, and rang up nearly $1.7 billion in 1998. It was, however, rated PG-13.

1996 RELEASES

INDEPENDENCE DAY

(20th Century Fox)
Rating: PG-13
Release date: July 3, 1996
Running time: 145 minutes
Genre: sci-fi thriller
Director: Roland Emmerich
Producer: Dean Devlin
Stars: Will Smith, Bill Pullman, Jeff Goldblum
Budget: $70 million
Gross: $306.1 million domestic + $440.0 million international = $746.1 million cumulative gross

TWISTER

(Warner Bros.)
Rating: PG-13
Release date: May 10, 1996
Running time: 117 minutes
Genre: action-adventure
Director: Jan de Bont
Producers: Kathleen Kennedy, Ian Bryce, Michael Crichton

Stars: Bill Paxton, Helen Hunt
Budget: $85 million
Gross: $241.7 million domestic + $251.8 million international = $493.5 million cumulative gross

Mission: Impossible

(Paramount Pictures)
Rating: PG-13
Release date: May 22, 1996
Running time: 120 minutes
Genre: action-adventure
Director: Brian De Palma
Producers: Tom Cruise, Paula Wagner
Stars: Tom Cruise, Jean Reno
Budget: $65 million
Gross: $181 million domestic + $271.6 million international = $452.6 million cumulative gross

The Rock

(Buena Vista)
Rating: R
Release date: June 7, 1996
Running time: 129 minutes
Genre: action-thriller
Director: Michael Bay
Producers: Don Simpson, Jerry Bruckheimer
Stars: Nicolas Cage, Sean Connery, Ed Harris
Budget: $65 million
Gross: $134 million domestic + $195.3 million international = $329.3 million cumulative gross

The Hunchback of Notre Dame

(Buena Vista)
Rating: G
Release date: June 21, 1996
Running time: 86 minutes
Genre: animated musical
Directors: Gary Trousdale, Kirk Wise
Producer: Don Hahn
Budget: $70 million
Gross: $99.9 million domestic + $184.5 million international = $284.4 million cumulative gross

1997 RELEASES

The Lost World: Jurassic Park

(Universal Films)
Rating: PG-13
Release date: May 23, 1997
Running time: 134 minutes
Genre: sci-fi thriller
Director: Steven Spielberg
Producers: Gerald Molen, Colin Wilson
Stars: Jeff Goldblum, Vince Vaughn
Budget: $77 million
Gross: $229.1 million domestic + $382.3 million international = $611.4 million cumulative gross

Men in Black

(Sony Pictures Entertainment)
Rating: PG-13
Release date: July 2, 1997
Running time: 98 minutes
Genre: sci-fi-adventure-comedy
Director: Barry Sonnenfeld
Producers: Walter F. Parkes, Laurie MacDonald
Stars: Will Smith, Tommy Lee Jones
Budget: $85 million
Gross: $250 million domestic + $313 million international = $563 million cumulative gross

LIAR LIAR

(Universal Pictures)
Rating: PG-13
Release date: March 21, 1997
Running time: 87 minutes
Genre: comedy
Director: Tom Shadyac
Producer: Brian Grazer
Star: Jim Carrey
Budget: $65 million
Gross: $181.4 million domestic + $118.6 international = $300.0 million cumulative gross

AIR FORCE ONE

(Columbia Pictures)
Rating: R
Release date: July 25, 1997
Running time: 124 minutes
Genre: action-thriller
Director: Wolfgang Petersen
Producers: Wolfgang Petersen, Gail Katz, Armyan Bernstein, Jon Schestack
Stars: Harrison Ford, Gary Oldman
Budget: $75 million
Gross: $171.9 million domestic + $126.4 million international = $298.3 million cumulative gross

THE FIFTH ELEMENT

(Sony/Gaumont)
Rating: PG-13
Release date: May 9, 1997
Running time: 127 minutes
Genre: sci-fi
Director: Luc Besson
Producer: Patrice Ledoux
Stars: Bruce Willis, Gary Oldman
Budget: $90 million
Gross: $63.8 million domestic + $200.1 million international = $263.9 million cumulative gross

1998 RELEASES

TITANIC

(Paramount Pictures/ 20th Century Fox)
Rating: PG-13
Release date: December 19, 1997
Running time: 194 minutes
Genre: romantic-historical drama
Director: James Cameron
Producers: James Cameron, Jon Landau
Stars: Leonardo DiCaprio, Kate Winslet
Budget: $220 million
Gross: $600.7 million domestic + $1,209.0 million international = $1,809.7 million cumulative gross

SAVING PRIVATE RYAN

(DreamWorks Pictures/ Paramount Pictures)
Rating: R
Release date: July 24, 1998
Running time: 169 minutes
Genre: drama
Director: Steven Spielberg
Producers: Steven Spielberg, Ian Bryce, Mark Gordon, Gary Levinsohn
Stars: Tom Hanks, Matt Damon, Ed Burns
Budget: $65 million
Gross: $190.8 million domestic + $232.0 million international = $422.8 million cumulative gross

Armageddon

(Touchstone Pictures)
Rating: PG-13
Release date: July 1, 1998
Running time: 150 minutes
Genre: sci-fi thriller
Director: Michael Bay
Producers: Jerry Bruckheimer, Gale Anne Hurd, Michael Bay
Stars: Bruce Willis, Ben Affleck
Budget: $150 million
Gross: $201.5 million domestic + $262.8 million international = $464.3 million cumulative gross

Godzilla

(Sony Pictures Entertainment)
Rating: PG-13
Release date: May 20, 1998
Running time: 139 minutes
Genre: sci-fi thriller
Director: Roland Emmerich
Producer: Dean Devlin
Stars: Matthew Broderick, Jean Reno, Maria Pitillo
Budget: $120 million
Gross: $136.2 million domestic + $239.7 million international = $375.9 million cumulative gross

Deep Impact

(Paramount/DreamWorks)
Rating: PG-13
Release date: May 8, 1998
Running time: 120 minutes
Genre: sci-fi-disaster-drama
Director: Mimi Leder
Producers: Richard D. Zanuck, David Brown
Stars: Morgan Freeman, Téa Leoni, Elijah Wood
Budget: $85 million
Gross: $140.5 million domestic + $208.3 million international = $348.8 million cumulative gross

REPS INDEX
(Agents and Managers)

REPS

(Agents and Managers)

The following is an index of all the reps (agents or managers) listed throughout the biographical entries.

ARTISTS MANAGEMENT GROUP
9465 Wilshire Blvd. Suite 519
Beverly Hills, CA 90212
Phone: (310) 860-8000
Fax: (310) 271-9753

BRESLER-KELLY & ASSOCIATES
11550 West Olympic Blvd. Suite 510
Los Angeles, CA 90048
Phone: (310) 479-5611
Fax: (310) 479-3775

BRILLSTEIN-GREY ENTERTAINMENT
9150 Wilshire Blvd. Suite 350
Beverly Hills, CA 90212
Phone: (310) 275-6135
Fax: (310) 275-6180

CREATIVE ARTISTS AGENCY
9830 Wilshire Blvd.
Beverly Hills, CA 90212
Phone: (310) 288-4545
Fax: (310) 288-4800

ENDEAVOR AGENCY
9701 Wilshire Blvd.
Beverly Hills, CA 90212
Phone: (310) 248-2000
Fax: (310) 248-2020

THE GERNERT COMPANY
136 East 57th St.
New York, NY 10022
Phone: (212) 838-7777
Fax: (212) 838-6020

THE GERSH AGENCY
232 North Canon Dr.
Beverly Hills, CA 90210
Phone: (310) 274-6611
Fax: (310) 274-4035

GOLD/MILLER COMPANY
9220 Sunset Blvd. Suite 320
Los Angeles, CA 90069
Phone: (310) 278-8990
Fax: (310) 278-0288

HAROLD GREENE AGENCY
13900 Marquesas Way
Building C Suite 83
Marina Del Rey, CA 90292
Phone: (310) 823-5393
Fax: (310) 821-7440

Hofflund/Polone Management
9465 Wilshire Blvd. Suite 820
Beverly Hills, CA 90212
Phone: (310) 859-1971
Fax: (310) 859-7250

Independent Artists Management
7906 Wenwood Blvd. Suite B
Baton Rouge, LA 70809
Phone: (225) 926-9190
Fax: (225) 924-0149

Industry Entertainment
955 South Carrillo Dr. Suite 300
Los Angeles, CA 90048
Phone: (323) 954-9000
Fax: (323) 954-9009

International Creative Management
8942 Wilshire Blvd.
Beverly Hills, CA 90211
Phone: (310) 550-4000
Fax: (310) 550-4100

The Irv Schechter Company
9300 Wilshire Blvd. Suite 400
Beverly Hills, CA 90212
Phone: (310) 278-8070
Fax: (310) 278-6058

Malkin Management
465 South Beverly Dr. Third Floor
Beverly Hills, CA 90212
Phone: (310) 226-2555
Fax: (310) 226-2550

McQueeney Management
10279 Century Woods Dr.
Los Angeles, CA 90067
Phone: (310) 277-1882
Fax: (310) 788-0985

Paradigm Talent & Literary Agency
10100 Santa Monica Blvd. 25th Floor
Los Angeles, CA 90067
Phone: (310) 277-4400
Fax: (310) 277-7820

Rosenstone/Wender Agency
3 East 48th St.
New York, NY 10017
Phone: (212) 832-8330
Fax: (212) 759-4524

The Sanford-Gross Agency
1015 Gayley Ave. Suite 301
Los Angeles, CA 90024
Phone: (310) 208-2100
Fax: (310) 208-6704

3 Arts Entertainment
9460 Wilshire Blvd.
Beverly Hills, CA 90212
Phone: (310) 888-3200
Fax: (310) 888-3210

United Talent Agency
9560 Wilshire Blvd. Suite 500
Beverly Hills, CA 90212
Phone: (310) 273-6700
Fax: (310) 247-1111

William Morris Agency
151 El Camino Dr.
Beverly Hills, CA 90212
Phone: (310) 859-4000
Fax: (310) 859-4462

1325 Avenue of the Americas
New York, NY 10019
Phone: (212) 586-5100
Fax: (212) 246-3583

WRITERS & ARTISTS AGENCY
8383 Wilshire Blvd. Suite 550
Beverly Hills, CA 90211
Phone: (323) 866-0900
Fax: (323) 659-1985